SYLVIE BERMANN is a career diplomat and was the French ambassador to the United Kingdom between 2014 and 2017. She grew up in Lyon, and studied history at Paris-Sorbonne and then specialised in oriental languages. Later she studied at the Beijing Language and Culture University, where she had her first taste of diplomacy as a closely monitored exchange student after the end of the Cultural Revolution in 1976. She became the first female French ambassador to China in 2011. She was Director for the United Nations, International Organisations, Human Rights and Francophonie from 2005 to 2011. She also became the ambassador for France in Russia in 2017, before she retired from the French foreign ministry in 2020. In July 2021 she was appointed by OSCE as a mediator and coordinator of the political branch of the trilateral contact group in charge of the implementation of the Minsk agreement on Donbas.

COLIN McINTOSH, a UK national, is a retired lawyer and translator currently living in France. Born in Germany and raised in Scotland, he studied Law at the University of Edinburgh (LLB Hons) and the University of McGill in Canada (LLM). Soon after qualifying, he went to work at the Court of Justice of the European Communities in Luxembourg, first as Deputy Head of Personnel and then as part of a small team of lawyers undertaking background research for the judges. After five years, he moved to the Organisation for Economic Co-operation and Development (OECD) in Paris, working first in the Legal Affairs Section of the Nuclear Energy Agency and then, for many years, in the Translation Division. Here he combined translation and revision work with the duties of Registrar of the OECD's Administrative Tribunal. Retired since 2011, he continues to take on occasional translation work and to follow British politics from afar.

Au Revoir Britannia

SYLVIE BERMANN

TRANSLATED INTO ENGLISH BY COLIN McINTOSH

Luath Press Limited

EDINBURGH

www.luath.co.uk

First published in French by Editions Stock 2021

First published in English by Luath Press 2022

ISBN: 978-1-910022-53-5

The author's right to be identified as author of this book under the
Copyright, Designs and Patents Act 1988 has been asserted.

The paper used in this book is recyclable. It is made from low
chlorine pulps produced in a low energy, low emission manner
from renewable forests.

Printed and bound by Severnprint Ltd, Gloucester

Typeset in 11.5 point Sabon by Lapiz

Contents

Preface to the UK Edition

I AM DELIGHTED THAT my book, *Au Revoir Britannia,* has been published in English.

It was originally written in order to describe to my compatriots the astonishing period of Brexit as witnessed from my privileged position as Ambassador of France. I relayed what I had seen and, most importantly, heard, albeit without always revealing my sources. British readers will of course be familiar with the events described. The analysis, by a French diplomat who is both an Anglophile and a Europhile, is of the historic moment when a country enjoying enviable prosperity decided to change course overnight. I looked on as the United Kingdom, flourishing and self-confident, turned into a profoundly divided country where the prevailing atmosphere, tinged with xenophobia, was one of bitterness in which Europeans, and the French in particular, seemed to have become its enemies. The book also endeavoured to explain that, although the European Union had served as a catalyst in relation to existing – but until then, hidden – frustrations, there were many other factors at play as well. Additionally, I felt that France could perhaps learn lessons from this surge of populism.

More than five years have passed since the day in June 2016 that was a game changer for both the United Kingdom and the European Union. When I returned to London in the weeks preceding the lockdown, I was surprised to find, not that Brexit had become a reality now accepted by everyone since there was no alternative, but rather a fairly general feeling that because it had happened, it was difficult to fathom that there could have been a different outcome. Brexit had somehow become the country's destiny, to the point where I began to doubt my own recollections, detailed as they were, so historic had been the event.

The very great majority of those with whom I had come into contact before the referendum, whether in London or in the provinces, Remainers or Brexiteers (including Boris Johnson himself) did not believe Brexit would happen. One member of Parliament, after listing all the reasons why he felt the United Kingdom should leave, told me he knew very well the British would remain in the EU, adding with a mischievous air that they would continue to annoy the Europeans, and wondered whether the latter were sure they really wanted them to stay. When, 15 days after the referendum, I reminded him of his unequivocal opinions, he confessed he would have bet everything he owned that Remain would win the day. During an interview I gave on the occasion of the fifth anniversary of Brexit, the French-speaking Belgian channel, RTBF, rebroadcast the BBC's announcement of the result, describing it as extraordinary and a veritable earthquake. This took me back to the state of shock we were all in at the time.

If I was so astonished by the result it was because almost everyone, from pollsters to bookmakers – including politicians and the media – was convinced that Brexit would not happen. Although I did not visit the Nissan factory in Sunderland, which turned out to be the epicentre of the Leave vote, I did go to the plant where Airbus wings were manufactured and where there was a very strong French presence. It is true that there were mixed feelings there about how they perceived the European Union and how they intended to vote. I made a point of travelling around the provinces as often as possible, when I was not obliged by my work to remain in the capital, but London, one of the stellar capitals of the world, enjoys an almost vampire-like dominance in the country. I confess that I did not see much of the suburbs, but in London itself, I was constantly meeting with members of Parliament from all sides. And unlike their French counterparts, British MPS return every weekend to their constituencies in order to 'take the pulse' of their constituents and keep in touch with local concerns. How is it that they failed completely to pick up on the prevailing mood? And what is to be said about David Cameron's conviction that he would win the referendum?

I finished writing my book in early January 2021, but subsequent developments have done nothing to alter its conclusions or the many interrogations raised within it. When analysing history in the making, it is difficult to adopt a standpoint of detached objectivity. Nothing is ever definitively settled. Since my book was published, several excellent volumes written by knowledgeable British observers – such as Philip Stephens' *Britain Alone: the Path From Suez to Brexit* (2021),[1] or Peter Ricketts' *Hard Choices* (2021)[2] – have analysed the underlying causes of Brexit and tried, as far as possible, to predict what will happen next.

Success or failure? A good decision or a mistake? Even Dominic Cummings, the architect of Brexit, has been openly asking himself these questions. In any event, as things stand, it is difficult to identify any advantages that Brexit has brought. On the contrary, the United Kingdom now has a lower ranking in the classification of G20 countries; a drastic reduction in trade with Europe; the need for companies to set up subsidiaries on the continent; and serious difficulties for fishermen and farmers, as well as for small and medium-sized enterprises in general. The City has been overtaken by the Amsterdam stock exchange as regards share transactions; there is an increase in bureaucracy rather than the hoped for reduction – the list goes on. The rush to conclude free trade agreements with the rest of the world has resulted in 'cut, copy and paste' versions of the ones previously concluded by the European Union. The one exception is the agreement concluded with Australia, hailed as the UK's first sovereignty agreement. But it has been calculated that this agreement will result in an increase in Gross Domestic Product (GDP) of between only 0.01 and 0.02 per cent, while its terms are favourable to the Australians at the expense of Britain's livestock farmers. Strangely, a new minister, Jacob Rees-Mogg has been appointed in order to seek opportunities from Brexit. Naturally, the United Kingdom has many assets which could enable it to bounce back but whatever happens, the consequences of Brexit will be a loss in terms not only of relative earning power but also of geopolitical influence.

It is of course true that the United Kingdom's COVID-19 vaccination campaign has been a success but, contrary to what is claimed by some, this has nothing to do with Brexit – matters of health fall under national jurisdiction. The campaign itself began, and massive orders for vaccines were made, while the United Kingdom was in the transition period and therefore still bound by EU rules. The European Union, slow to get started and not benefitting from the vaccines produced in British laboratories, opted for a policy of solidarity in order to ensure that the smallest European countries were also able to acquire vaccines, thus enabling a return to free movement. The EU, which has vaccinated more than half its population, has also exported half the doses produced in Europe to developing countries, thereby becoming the world's pharmacy at a time when it has become evident that the virus will not disappear until citizens of all the world's countries have been vaccinated.

'Global Britain' is having difficulty making its mark: the aircraft carrier *Queen Elizabeth*, sent with great fanfare into the Indo–Pacific region, avoided the Taiwan Strait so as not to provoke China; the G7 chaired in June 2021 by Boris Johnson was perturbed by the key question of implementation of the Northern Ireland Protocol. Just before the summit, Joe Biden asked for assurance that the agreement would be complied with. Biden also publicly stated his appreciation for the European Union as a strong and vibrant entity – clearly size does matter. What is at stake – over and above preserving peace in Northern Ireland where tensions still run high and, for the European Union, protecting the single market – is the value that can be put on the United Kingdom's signature.

The United Kingdom's relationship with Europe has been deeply and permanently affected. Brexit is by no means an amicable, mutual consent divorce and there is a great deal of bitterness on both sides. As far as the Europeans are concerned, there are many other priorities to be addressed: the implementation of a recovery plan; the migrant crisis; a new transatlantic agenda; the complex relationship with China, Russia and Turkey; and agreeing on a strategic compass. On the British side there is the normal and legitimate wish to make a success of Brexit. As they say in Britain, 'we are where we are'. But there is a tendency, with such an obsessional approach, to want to blot Europe out, as shown by the extremely marginal place allocated to it in the Integrated Review of spring 2021. This borders on the absurd when the Government boasts about an agreement to allow British performers to circulate freely in Lichtenstein, whereas this same right, generously offered by the European Union, was turned down flat by London. Or again, when armed British patrol boats threaten French fishing vessels off Jersey, where I had been so warmly welcomed '*comme chez moi*' when I was Ambassador in London (and where the courts apply the Norman law as studied by the island's lawyers in the University of Caen). All these episodes demonstrate that it will take time to rebuild relations with the European Union as a whole and individually with France, Germany and other partners. For rebuild they must since, as Napoleon said, 'the only thing that doesn't change in history is geography' and our interests and values remain close in a world dominated by continent-sized states, some of them autocratic regimes.

Isn't absolute sovereignty an illusion today given the global challenges existing in an increasingly uncertain multipolar world?

Since publication of my book in France in January 2021, a major event has occurred, a real game-changer in Europe and on the world stage: the war of aggression launched by Vladimir Putin against Ukraine.

The Russian President, isolated for almost two years in a psychological ghetto – as well as a physical one because of his fear of COVID – was apparently brooding over his old obsessions: the first being the denial of the existence of Ukraine as a nation; the second, the presence of NATO on the borders of Russia which he considers to be a threat to national security. During this period, he interacted almost exclusively with a small entourage who shared his obsessions or who were, at any rate, afraid to contradict him. After witnessing the American debacle in Kabul in August 2021, he was convinced that the West was weak. Joe Biden had said prior to the invasion that the US wouldn't interfere, so Putin no doubt thought his time had come.

To most people, this war was literally unthinkable, and up until the last moment, the authorities and people of Ukraine refused to countenance the possibility of a major invasion targeting Kyiv. As the moderator of the OSCE (Organization for Security and Co-operation in Europe) and coordinator of the political working group of the TCG (Trilateral Contact Group), responsible for implementation of the Minsk agreement,[i] I was witness to this myself since I was in Kyiv three weeks before the war and kept in contact with my Ukrainian counterparts till the very day before the invasion was launched. Although cyber warfare has become almost commonplace, nobody thought there would be a conventional conflict in Europe along the lines of the Second World War.

It is, of course, a tragedy for the Ukrainian people but neither is it in the interests of Russia, which has much to lose. Putin wanted to turn Ukraine into a vassal state and make it pro-Russian whereas, in fact, he reinforced the feeling of national identity and provoked widespread hatred of the Russian people. He wanted to weaken NATO, but instead he gave it a *raison d'être*. He hoped to divide the EU, which he despises, but instead succeeded in unifying it. It is worth noting that the EU, for the first time, decided unanimously and swiftly not only to give humanitarian as well as financial assistance and impose unprecedented sanctions, but also to provide defensive weapons in order to help Ukraine exercise its right to defend itself.

As this book goes to press, the war is not over but European countries from now on will have to think the unthinkable. Even if it appears (so far) to have been something of a bluff, there has

---

[i] The Minsk agreement was formed to facilitate peace in the Ukraine by creating dialogue with Russia.

been an implicit threat of resorting to nuclear weapons. The strategic compass adopted in March 2022 by the EU has been adapted to this new environment. It will inevitably require more brainstorming and also more concertation with the UK, which cannot be satisfied with simply following the American position. This war took place in Europe and it is Europe that will suffer many of the consequences: sanctions, vulnerability of neighbouring countries, refugees and so forth. In these circumstances, even if it is only a personal regret, and it is in the past, I cannot help thinking that the EU would have been stronger with the participation of London and that the UK would have greater influence if it were still a member of the EU.

After the war, there will inevitably be negotiations with Russia with a view at least to ensuring strong guarantees regarding a possible status of neutrality for Ukraine, and more generally to design a new architecture for security in Europe. In the longer run, 'the West' will also have to take greater account of 'the Rest', as they say in United Nations circles, meaning the largest part of the world – including China in particular which, although embarrassed by this war, will want to keep its partnership with Russia, knowing that it is still Washington's primary target. 'The Rest' also includes India, Pakistan, Brazil, South Africa and the 17 African countries that abstained in the vote condemning the Russian invasion in the UN General Assembly in March 2022, and which do not necessarily share our views on this new Cold War between democracies and autocracies

* * *

Anglophile through my love of British culture and humour and Europhile because the European Union serves as a multiplier of national power, I nonetheless retain my French identity which inevitably colours my vision of England and the United Kingdom. But I think that a vision from another standpoint, whether one agrees with it or not, is always instructive.

Introduction

IN LEWIS CARROLL'S 1865 classic, *Alice's Adventures in Wonderland,* the White Queen authorised Alice to tell six lies or believe 'six impossible things' before breakfast.[1] The fictional Queen would be pleased, as more than six lies were told during the referendum campaign on whether the United Kingdom should remain in the European Union, during which the subjects of her Gracious Majesty lived in a sort of make-believe world. Waking up on the morning after the referendum of 23 June 2016 was painful. But for all that, reality did not reclaim centre stage. The result was that, for the following three and a half years, the British were plunged into the absurd universe of *Alice in Wonderland,* or even *Monty Python.* There was veritable chaos, and often a political circus involving some highly colourful characters such as Speaker of the House of Commons John Bercow at Westminster, the so-called 'mother of parliaments'. His frequent shouts for 'ORDEEER' will go down in history.

On 1st April 2019, a comical event occurred when young ecological activists from Extinction Rebellion glued themselves, almost naked, to the windows of the Visitors' Gallery in the House of Commons during yet another inconclusive debate on Brexit. This gave rise to several sarcastic, or disenchanted, comments on social media – if only it was the most ridiculous or nonsensical thing to have taken place in this forum over the last five years.

Only the triumphant, and somewhat paradoxical, election in December 2019 of Boris Johnson – whose campaign slogan was 'Get Brexit Done' in a country where the polls gave a slight majority for remaining in the European Union – put an end to the debate once and for all.

Meanwhile, the world continued to move forward, the COVID pandemic bringing into focus some of the changing patterns of power.

When I arrived at the Court of St James in August 2014 – ambassadors are accredited to the Queen and not to the prime minister – quite a few British people told me I would be bored after the years I had spent in China where I witnessed the accession to power of Xi Jinping and China's growing assertiveness on the international stage. The feeling was that I was coming back to a quiet, uneventful post in old Europe. To their great astonishment and amusement, I replied that I did not think I would be bored since the British were, in my eyes at least, as culturally different as the Chinese, if not more so. The royal family and the parade of monarchy; the Queen's hats; the pomp of the Tudors at Westminster; the judges in their powdered wigs; the 'old boys' clubs; horse racing at Ascot; the annual City Guild parades; cricket matches; the pubs; a myriad of accents, from Cockney to the very posh; the smell of fish and chips in the street; bookmakers; and, as always, the humour – all these 'so British' idiosyncrasies. All so well and entertainingly described in the 1930s and again the 1960s by a former attaché to the French Embassy in London, Paul Morand:[2]

> A Frenchman used to spending his holidays in Italy or Spain will, on crossing the Channel, be immediately transported into a foreign world where the urban landscapes and customs are so different from those of continental Europe – so near and yet so far, neighbours that in fact we know so little.

I was not, however, expecting to bear witness to a revolution – to live through history in the making. This is a period that will be remembered 50 or 100 years from now and which has indeed already inspired many novels such as *Middle England* by Jonathan Coe,[3] who captured so well the spirit of the time; or even in the form of parodies of quintessential English children's literature: *Five on Brexit Island*,[4] and *Alice in Brexitland*,[5] the latter with the clear warning of 'You don't have to be mad to live here but it helps....'

In the autumn of 2019, with the final decision on the departure of the United Kingdom approaching, two new books, resolutely hostile to Brexit, expressed the anger of their authors. In a short, Kafkaesque dystopia entitled *The Cockroach*, which also evokes Jonathan Swift, Ian McEwan describes the metamorphosis of Prime Minister Boris Johnson into a cockroach 'in order to pursue "reversalism", the most futile and masochistic ambition ever imagined in the history of the British Isles, a long journey back to a mere shadow of what we were.'[6] John le Carré, himself a committed European, put Brexit, which he thought to be pure folly, at the heart of his latest spy novel, *Agent Running in the Field*.[7]

The result of the referendum in June 2016 on whether the United Kingdom should remain in the European Union did indeed constitute a revolution in this *nation de boutiquier,* (nation of shopkeepers) to use Napoleon's disdainful expression (but one that was willingly assumed by members of the Tory Party, for whom money and therefore economic interests were supposed to take precedence over all other considerations). Emotion, in fact, prevailed over reason; ideology and dogmatism over pragmatism. It overturned the perception and the conviction of the country's political leaders that their compatriots were viscerally attached to the status quo.

For British commentators, the break with Europe brought to mind past occasions when the country's destiny had changed radically. While the most common reference was to the Suez crisis in 1956, some went back to the Blitz and the Battle of Britain in 1940 – I even heard a comparison with the American War of Independence, which demonstrates the depth of the trauma. The word 'tragedy' was frequently used. An unusual revolution nevertheless since, unlike the case of the election of Donald Trump in the United States, the 'revolutionaries' did not accede to power immediately. The summer of 2016 saw a succession of winners, struggling to come to terms with their victory, stabbing each other in the back, day after day, in a series of burlesque events worthy of Shakespeare.

It was, in fact, a Conservative former Remainer (albeit a rather half-hearted one) who became prime minister. *The Times* published a memorable cartoon by Peter Brookes where she is shown in her signature pointed leopard print shoes, stepping over the bodies of her rivals lying in a pool of blood, each one having been stabbed.[8]

The victory of Theresa May, without the need for any campaign since she had no challengers, was something of a relief, since reason seemed to have won the day over the impending collapse of the political establishment. But since she had not been a Brexiteer during the referendum campaign, Theresa May now felt the need to overcompensate in order to prove that she was the right person to lead the country in its divorce from the European Union. Initially, her decision to appoint the three 'Brexit Musketeers' to senior, and to some degree competing, posts was seen as a stroke of genius, and not without humour. There was Foreign Secretary Boris Johnson, Secretary of State for Exiting the European Union David Davis, and Secretary of State for International Trade Liam Fox. In this way, she seemed to have pushed their backs to the wall, condemning them to fail in an impossible mission.

The new Prime Minister, on every possible occasion, repeated the now-famous (and sometimes ridiculed) mantra, 'Brexit means Brexit.' Under pressure from her European partners – particularly France, seemingly impatient to wind up divorce proceedings – she invoked the now-famous Article 50 of the EU Treaty thereby triggering the withdrawal procedure on 30 March 2017, before there was any clear decision as to the mechanism, strategy, or even definition of Brexit. The two-year countdown was set in motion even though the French and German elections, scheduled for the spring and early autumn of 2017 respectively, could have been used as a pretext for giving more time for preparation.

I shall never forget the evening or the sleepless night of the referendum which, in my diplomatic correspondence preceding the results of the vote, I had termed 'the longest night'. As far as the prediction I was expected to give was concerned, I concluded on the cautious note expressed by the Remainers I had met in the days immediately preceding: 'Fingers crossed.'

The financial director of the Remain campaign, Roland Rudd, had invited me to watch the proceedings in a St James's club. A few ministers, businessmen and lawyers were there as well as my opposite numbers from Germany, Italy and Ireland – the last-mentioned having been very active in the campaign both because of the one million Irish people living in the United Kingdom, with the right to vote, and also because of the risks of Brexit for Ireland. Everyone was relaxed. After some fluctuations in the polls in the preceding weeks, the shock caused by the tragic murder some days earlier of the Remainer Member of Parliament for Labour Jo Cox, in a climate of nationalistic hate and exaltation, seemed to have calmed things down and closed the ranks. Both Remainers and Brexiteers were convinced, the former with satisfaction and the latter with despair, that the result would be in favour of remaining in the EU. At 10pm, the informal exit polls, commissioned by the City, gave 52 per cent in favour of Remain. Nigel Farage, the leader of the UK Independence Party (UKIP), at this point conceded defeat while asserting that this would not be the end of the debate, given the narrow margin of victory for the Remainers (he said that it was not over since the Remainers had [only] 52 per cent, so the matter was not settled and he was not going to stay quiet). Eighty members of Parliament, from both sides then wrote to David Cameron to ask him to stay on as prime minister, whatever the result.

There was a similar atmosphere in Number 10 – the Prime Minister's unassuming residence in Downing Street – as David Cameron's close associates had been invited for a supper to celebrate his victory, given that Director of Politics and Communications Craig Oliver (reported that no negative signals had been picked up during the day.[9] It was only after midnight that the Prime Minister texted him to ask, 'How worried should we be?'

The Chancellor of the Exchequer George Osborne left Downing Street briefly around 10.30pm to join us and we all congratulated each other, even though the Chancellor feared that the result might, in fact, be closer. Asked, nevertheless, to say a few words, he said that this proved that it was possible to discuss the European Union in this country and, turning towards me, that I could transmit this message to Paris. I didn't have the time.

What happened next is well-known. After returning to the French Residence in Kensington Palace Gardens, I watched the results in real time on television with members of my team. The first results were in line with expectations, with 96 per cent in favour of Remain in Gibraltar. But things quickly began to change since, even in places where the Remain vote won, the margin was smaller than predicted. Then the storm broke around 1.00am in Sunderland, an industrial city of the North East, home of the Nissan complex (the leading local employer) where, against all expectations, the Leave vote won by a large majority. Scenes of the exultant victors embracing each other were shown over and over again in the early morning. I decided to snatch an hour's sleep, set the alarm for 3am and to go back to bed if the results were reassuring. They were not. Even though Paola, my young colleague in charge of European affairs, tried to reassure us by pointing out that the London and Manchester results were not yet in, the party was over. Paul, my *Chef de Cabinet,* arrived at 5.00am in a black cab – the driver, a Remainer, had confessed that he had not voted since he thought Remain was going to win. At this juncture, Senator Fabienne Keller, vice-chair of the Commission for European Affairs, arrived. She had agreed to spend the night on Sky News and comment on the results from a French point of view alongside the father of Boris, Stanley Johnson, who was wearing his environmental (and especially European) convictions on his T-shirt. The shock was huge and the coffee and croissants left a bitter taste in my mouth.

Many subjects of Her Majesty who had gone to bed confident were even more stupefied. While Brexiteers couldn't believe their ears, some Remainers, though perhaps not prone to outbursts of emotion, were in tears. In the morning, many people, including some amongst the so-called victors, looked distinctly haggard.

The week following, the think tanks were in full swing, organising early breakfast meetings in one club or another in an attempt to understand. In fact, for more than five years, the British have tried hard to make sense of what had happened, rerunning the film over and over, wondering how it had come to this. 'WTF' (*What the fuck*) was the expressive and provocative title of the book by journalist and political editor, Robert Peston.[10] There were many who remained, for a long time, in denial, in mourning or – for the most courageous – in resistance mode. Some hoped that it would be possible to reverse the decision by way of a second referendum on the outcome of the negotiations. This became more likely when Theresa May lost her majority in Parliament and her authority over her Cabinet following the surprise result of the early general election she called for on 8 June 2017. This was followed by resignations from the Cabinet after the Chequers meeting of July 2018 and then the setbacks in the House of Commons, which continued until a few weeks, even days, before the scheduled date of departure.

The country became obsessed with a single subject to the exclusion of all others: Brexit at breakfast, Brexit at lunch, Brexit at dinner (reminiscent in some ways of conversations at tables in France at the time of the Dreyfus affair). I was able to observe this at the Residence, where my guests replayed the match over and over again using the same arguments, expressing the same anger and the same intolerance. The country was deeply divided: between its constituent nations, metropolitan and rural areas, social classes, ethnic minorities, parties, generations, even families. Reports circulated of an increase in petitions for divorce and in the number of best friends falling out, as well as of grandchildren who no longer spoke to their grandparents, whom they accused of stealing their future.

Demons had been let loose; xenophobia and racism legitimised. There were instances of insults, intimidation and death threats being made on the street and more visibly on social media, where internet trolls gave vent to their feelings without restraint or any of the reserve for which the British are renowned. Residents from Europe no longer felt welcome in a country where some had lived for more than 20 years. Some said that they went from being happy and well-integrated Londoners on 23 June 2016, to foreigners the next day. In the United Kingdom – a model of representative democracy and fair play admired throughout the world, the country of Burke, critic of the follies of the French Revolution of 1789 and its clean slate approach – terms such as 'enemies of the people' or 'saboteurs', reminiscent rather of *La Terreur* following the French Revolution, or of Stalin's reign of terror, made the front page of the *Daily Mail* on 4 November 2016, alongside photos of the accused. These included the highest authorities of the land: ministers, members of Parliament and judges who had, until then, enjoyed great respect.

But was it, in fact, the European Union that was the root of the referendum defeat, or was it a convenient and obvious scapegoat? Ironically, the day following, 'EU' was the most searched term on the internet. What was this institution that they had just decided to leave?[i] Many people had, in fact, no idea.

A few years earlier, although not enjoying particularly strong support, the European Union came only ninth or tenth on the list of

---

[i] General de Gaulle once referred to it as a *'machin'*, a 'thing'.

concerns of the British public. I remember a journey taken in 2005 by the Political and Security Committee of the European Union (chaired at the time by the United Kingdom and where I represented France) on an RAF plane from Brussels which landed at the Northwood military base. After a moment of panic on seeing the European flag fluttering next to the Union Jack at the airport, the UK Ambassador breathed a sigh of relief, remarking that luckily it couldn't be seen from the street. This was perhaps the tacit consensus, that membership of the EU should not be seen from the street. Otherwise, everything was going well. The Government had, over two years, drawn up a detailed and rigorous report – since forgotten, of course – on the various competencies in all areas of the European project, a report which concluded that the system served the interests of the United Kingdom perfectly. However, by linking the European Union to immigration (a subject of primary concern to the British) and blaming the principle of the free movement of workers imposed by membership for the arrival of nearly one million Polish nationals after the enlargement of the union, which was encouraged, it may be said, by Tony Blair, Nigel Farage was able to use the EU as a scapegoat. This played an important role in the referendum even though the main target, as expressed by many partisans of Brexit, seemed to be non-white immigrants, whether from Africa or elsewhere. Such immigration was often from Commonwealth countries and therefore had nothing to do with the EU principle of the free movement of workers.

The greatest possible confusion prevailed, opening the door to all sorts of lies, for example the supposed tens of millions of Turks – most of the Turkish population in fact – who were suddenly going to invade the United Kingdom following an accession, which wasn't even on the agenda, and over which London had a right of veto. In addition to this, by an unfortunate coincidence, the year 2015 saw the peak of the refugee crisis in Europe.

The United Kingdom was then the champion, and even embodiment, of successful globalisation; the wind fully in its sails, the most dynamic economy of the G7, its capital a new world city after the success of the Olympic Games, self-confident and in many ways more creative than New York. It was the financial capital of Europe and the world; capital of international arbitration and law; epicentre of the world's leading media, like the *Financial Times*, *The Economist* and the BBC; and the European headquarters of American, Middle Eastern and Asian companies. How did this country, one whose influence in Brussels had been decisive, that had the temerity to roll out the red carpet for French entrepreneurs and that, in October 2015, Xi Jinping had chosen as the gateway to Europe at the dawn of a golden era – how did it come to scupper itself in this way?

David Cameron attempted to convince people that the United Kingdom did indeed have the best of both worlds – access to the single market, which it had helped to create without the constraints of the Schengen rules on travel or the single currency – but he failed in his attempt. What's more, the UK had just succeeded in obtaining additional and not insignificant concessions from its European partners. One day, in a conference organised by the French Chamber of Great Britain, an Englishman asked what picture Brexit conjured up for me. The one that came to my mind was the recurring scene in *Astérix and Obélix* in which pirates, noticing the two heroes approaching in the distance, begin furiously to destroy their ship that they had only just finished repairing and making good as new. The cartoon following is that of the same pirates clinging onto a plank in the middle of the ocean saying bitterly, 'Now we don't even need the Gaulois to make us look ridiculous.'

David Cameron, who should have chaired the EU in triumph in the second quarter of 2017, will go down in history as the prime minister who took his country out of the EU 'by accident', as the Speaker of the House of Commons said one day to a delegation of French parliamentarians. Was it then an inevitable accident waiting to happen, as claimed by some? Or a campaign that failed to connect with the real issues given that the Prime Minister's main objective was to get on with the next phase of bringing his party together? Because the irony is that the whole Brexit affair was all to do with the toxic situation in the Tory Party, caused by a few who were virulently Europhobic. Convinced that he had the opportunity to settle this old quarrel, which had cost the Conservatives so dearly electorally, once and for all, David Cameron led a somewhat lacklustre campaign, concentrating rather on what was, to him, the more significant 'second round' (as did Lionel Jospin in France in 2002). He took his adversaries on with one hand tied behind his back, without really countering their arguments, failing to understand that his abstract slogan that Britain would be 'stronger, safer and better off' in the EU didn't have the same emotional impact as the Brexiteers' promise of taking back control or 'independence day'. Not to mention their flagrant lies such as the emblematic sum of £350 million painted on the red bus driven around the country by Boris Johnson. This was supposed to represent the amount paid every week to the EU and it was claimed it could be paid instead to the National Health Service (NHS), a veritable sacred cow in the United Kingdom.

Was this result inevitable at the dawning of an era of populism exploiting the frustrations of those in the North East and the Midlands who felt left behind by globalisation, with the concomitant rejection of experts whose opinions were given no more importance than those of the most ignorant Internaut? The result was a loss of confidence in institutions, the blind faith in the opinion expressed by the next man in the pub. Were the social networks used in a more expert and cynical fashion by the partisans of Brexit? Notably through Cambridge Analytica, a company set up by Stephen Bannon from the American anti-establishment extreme right, that analyses, or more exactly collects, data.

Was it a vote by a racist people? An identity reflex in the face of globalisation that they failed to properly understand? A protest vote by the people against the elite, as has often been said? Or a manipulation of the people by the elite, or certain sections thereof?

It was, in reality, a battle between the elite. Would Brexit have happened without Boris Johnson? This archetypical English intellectual – eccentric, truculent, paradoxical and sympathetic – legitimised in the eyes of many what had until then been solely the position of the nationalist party UKIP and of a minority of hard-line backbenchers, fanatically Europhobic since the Thatcher era. In fact all of them were educated in the same universities and the same schools, with the same codes – Oxford, Cambridge and, above all, the prestigious Eton College, of which 19 British prime ministers were former pupils. There indeed exists an English pudding served in summer at Wimbledon and in the Clubs that bears the evocative name 'Eton Mess'. Legend has it that this was the result of a pavlova being accidentally turned upside down at a picnic and then hastily rearranged any which way by the pupils. A mixture of strawberries, meringue and whipped cream (rather tasty, from a strictly gourmand point of view), it provides an obvious metaphor for Brexit to judge by the confusion surrounding its meaning and content more than five years after the referendum.

The visceral Europhobia of the Brexiteers is based on nostalgia for a country and a world that no longer exist – the British Empire ruling the waves; the Commonwealth supposedly united around the Queen, whereas the Australians and New Zealanders look rather towards Beijing, and the Canadians towards Washington; the 'little Englander' attitude of those who consider themselves to be English rather than British; or the 'Anglosphere' preference for encouraging competent Australian immigrants rather than supposedly 'underqualified' European ones. Many British people are convinced that the United Kingdom was the only country to resist invasion by the Nazis, that it won the Second World War single-handedly and that the spirit of Dunkirk or the Blitz will continue to save the country against all-comers. Added to this is the illusion of a 'special relationship' with Washington whereas, at best, the United Kingdom is the junior partner of a country and of a leader with whom it had not, for four years, enjoyed shared values. This last point was illustrated, on the British side, by the large-scale demonstrations by young people in London against a proposed state visit by Donald Trump in 2017 and by the refusal of the Speaker of the Commons to welcome the President to the Westminster Parliament. After further hostile demonstrations were banned, a helium balloon depicting a fat, pink baby was hoisted above the city, complete with a large slick of blonde hair and a nappy attached by a safety pin, while official meetings were restricted to Windsor Castle or Chequers (the country residence of Britain's prime ministers). On the American side, Trump's incessant bullying conditions for signing a free trade agreement with London, as well as the bipartisan support given to Ireland by the American Congress (proof of a real, special relationship with that country), demonstrated the unequal nature of US–UK relations.

In spite of this, Brexiteers continue to maintain the illusion that Churchill's choice between the wider world and the continent of Europe is still valid today. The United Kingdom has, in any event, now lost the role of a bridge between America and Europe while the much-vaunted Global Britain, supposedly a replacement for membership of the EU, is wishful thinking given that Germany's trade with China, India and many other countries is worth three or four times as much as Britain's. This indeed is proof that nothing was stopping the United Kingdom from being a successful trading nation while still a member of the EU – by what miracle would leaving the European Union improve matters? As for taking back control over foreign policy, which Brexiteers were so keen to promote, London has hardly had the time or the resources to put this into practice.

The new American President's team has clearly signalled that there will not be a special relationship with the United Kingdom. Considering Brexit to be an historic mistake and – given his Irish roots in particular – strongly attached to the Good Friday

Agreement, Joe Biden had already made clear that he would never accept a free trade agreement with the United Kingdom if Boris Johnson tried to contravene provisions of the Good Friday Agreement in his negotiations with the European Union. What's more, Joe Biden has been severely critical of Boris Johnson himself, reportedly calling him Donald Trump's 'physical and emotional clone'.[11] Lastly, he let it be known through his staff (who have nicknamed Johnson 'Mini-Trump') that he would not forget the racist comments about Barack Obama, when Johnson claimed that the latter's partially Kenyan heritage explained his aversion to the British Empire (and therefore to Brexit). The least that can be said is that relations between London and Washington did not get off to the best of starts.

During the referendum campaign, Europeans and European institutions were reduced to silence. Brussels was paralysed and the Commission, which wisely refrained from passing new directives so as to avoid the recurrent criticism of regulatory inflation, refrained from comment. The Germans, with the possible exception of their finance minister, Wolfgang Schaüble, took immense care – as was confided to me by my German counterpart in London – to avoid being accused of trying to obtain, through the EU, what they had not succeeded in achieving in the Second World War. The French, considered as having 'given in' to the Third Reich, were accused of being ready to capitulate again to the Fourth Reich as constituted by the European Union under German domination.

These were comments I read and heard many times in response to the statements I made on television, the radio, or in the newspapers, emphasising France's wish to see the United Kingdom remain at our side in Europe since its departure would constitute a lose-lose situation for our two countries that were almost twins – practically the same population, the same status in the world, nuclear powers both, permanent members of the Security Council and capable of military projection. The UK is a country that shares our values and with which we have fought, side by side, for the last 200 years. A significant fact – together, France and the United Kingdom draft 70 per cent of the resolutions of the UN Security Council. France, alone, will now be responsible for representing the interests of 450 million European citizens. But the English in particular cannot stand being told what to do, as was shown by the backlash against Barack Obama's statement that should it go ahead with Brexit, the United Kingdom would be at the back of the queue as regards the negotiation of a free trade agreement. As for the tradition of 'French bashing' – which is always waiting in the wings, ready to take centre stage at a moment's notice, especially in difficult times – it incited us also to caution.

We will, in fact, all be losers since, against the giant continent-sized states that dominate today – the United States and China, and perhaps tomorrow, Russia, India and Brazil – it is absolutely necessary to oppose a critical mass, whether for trade negotiations or in terms of influence. Until the emergence of the COVID pandemic gave rise to *real* solidarity between Paris and Berlin, the tandem functioned with great difficulty. Never, in fact, had relations between the two been so strained as when London was no longer in the picture. The three-way relationship made it possible to join forces with the British, notably with regard to defence and security, in order to draw in the Germans. At a geopolitical level, in addition to its military resources, the United Kingdom has connections with African and Commonwealth countries, as does France with French-speaking ones.

We have to be realistic – the size of the United Kingdom as a mid-ranking power, though of course with other assets, is equivalent to little more than half the Chinese province of Guangdong. There is, therefore, no way forward other than by constructing Europe. In spite of some growing Euroscepticism, the other member states clearly understood this following the British referendum. Far from creating the feared domino effect, the departure of the United Kingdom has, in fact, served to strengthen ties between remaining nations. In 2016, a cartoon went viral on the internet, showing a 'domino defect' with the United Kingdom falling flat on its face, alone, while the others remained standing.

The story of Brexit could be told through such cartoons, a wonderful and thriving British tradition, as old as it is unmistakable. Humour abounding always, even if rather black in these post-Brexit days.

Given that Europe remained united, the negotiations were somewhat one-sided. The United Kingdom – convinced of the talent of its negotiators and of its traditional ability to divide and rule – was confident of having its cake and eating it too, as recorded in the notes of a young trainee which were captured on film by a photographer as participants came out of a meeting in the Foreign Office. A photomontage of Theresa May telephoning Sky News to announce that she was giving up her subscription but wished to continue to benefit from the services of the channel perfectly summed up this state of mind. To Michel Bernier and the 27 who kept repeating that the United Kingdom could not expect better treatment outside the club than in, that cherry-picking would not be allowed, there could not be rights without obligations. Theresa May, as in the sketch by Fernand Reynaud, kept on asking for two croissants.[ii]

A certain British minister shamelessly complained about the 'gangster' methods used by the European leaders in their desire to punish the United Kingdom. The intention imputed to the Europeans, and especially the French, to punish the United

---

[ii] Fernand Reynaud ordered a coffee with milk, and two croissants, from a waiter in a café. The waiter replied that they had run out of croissants. 'No matter', he said, 'I'll have a black coffee and two croissants.' 'But sir, I told you we have no more croissants.' The sketch continues with a glass of milk, a hot chocolate… and always two croissants.

Kingdom is a pure invention on the part of Brexiteers who act as though they had been asked to leave and claim that the British were being targeted, whereas they brought this punishment upon themselves. They don't seem able to understand that the European Union is based on rules of law that it has no intention of modifying to benefit a country that has decided to leave. Paradoxically, British leaders, who lost no opportunity to explain that they had joined the EU solely in order to access the common (now single) market and rejected all the other aspects, decided after the referendum to leave this same single market. They decided to do so while trying, at least initially, to stay as close as possible to the other policies such as those in relation to justice, security and defence, which they found useful, and even hoped to join several programmes at the risk of having to adhere to rules that they would not have been involved in drafting.

Those who are not Brexit fanatics know that there is no such thing as a 'good' Brexit. They know that it will cost the country a lot in terms of national influence and that the sacrosanct 'people' who listened to the sirens of the Brexiteers will be those who will suffer the most, especially if the result is a 'Singapore-on-Thames' (the tax haven dreamed about by the most extreme) even if, especially given the COVID pandemic, this is not the most likely outcome today. Perhaps, if they were to have avoided suffering the consequences, the least well-off should have paid more attention to the slogan 'Brexit is for the Rich'. In fact, the somewhat rare company directors who were ardent supporters of Brexit, lost no time in transferring their head offices out of the United Kingdom – including James Dyson, the maker of vacuum cleaners, who relocated Dyson to Singapore.

On the other side, during the three uncertain years following the referendum, never had there been so many EU flags flown in the streets of London and other large Northern cities; flags flown by those, in particular the young, who rejected this fateful decision to divorce.

Weary of the never-ending strife, plagued by uncertainty, anxious, above all, to prevent the election of the Labour bogeyman Jeremy Corbyn – a figure stuck in the ideology of the 1970s – the majority of the British voted for Boris Johnson and for Brexit in 2019, since his campaign slogan, 'Get Brexit done' left no room for ambiguity. But this did not mean that relations with Brussels had been settled. In the autumn of 2020, the second phase of the negotiations, delayed because of the health crisis, gave rise to further acrimony.

During the first phase, aware that they had become an international laughing stock because of their indecision and lack of coherence, the British showed a certain reserve in their dealings with the EU. With the election of an apparently strong and charismatic leader like Boris Johnson, they reverted to type and asked again for special treatment – to have their cake and eat it. A former Remainer was prompted to say that the United Kingdom was not a third state country, or a state like any other – 'We are not Malta or Austria' – forgetting, once again, that no one asked them to leave, that their decision brought consequences with it and that solidarity is owed to members of the club, both large and small. As for Boris Johnson, he tried an enormous bluff by repudiating his signature and his country's word, calling into question the 'fantastic agreement', to use his own hyperbole, that he had concluded a year before.

But just before Christmas, drawing the conclusions of the election of Joe Biden, which was not favourable to him, and while thousands of lorries stranded in Kent gave a taste of what Brexit without an agreement would be like, the Prime Minister ended up making concessions previously deemed unacceptable, in relation to competition and fishing. This was in order to avoid the shock of a 'no deal', considering that if he could, nevertheless, affirm that the United Kingdom had recovered sovereignty over its waters, its money and its laws, then there was no loss of face.

Reminiscent of the tennis ball in Woody Allen's film *Match Point*, which could easily have fallen on the other side of the net, Brexit in fact turned out to be the first episode of the crisis in representative democracy caused by a groundswell that had been kept below the radar in other countries.

Commentators can, *a posteriori*, analyse the first weak signals of this movement to conclude that it was obvious or unavoidable, but this wasn't the case at the time. The second episode was no doubt the election of Donald Trump, highly unlikely right up until the last minute, and analysed the following day as a revolutionary protest by those who felt left behind by globalisation, a protest which profited a millionaire real estate developer. The similarities were very marked: a frustrated electorate; the methods employed, including the use of Cambridge Analytica; the shift towards the right-wing in the Republican Party in the United States and in the Conservative Party in the United Kingdom, amplified by the media controlled by Rupert Murdoch; and the exploitation of these frustrations by a populist leader. We paid only scant attention to the advance of populism in Hungary or Poland, countries that we generally think of as lacking in solid democratic traditions due to their history and for which we invented the term 'illiberal'. More striking is the conjunction of both left-wing and right-wing populism in Italy represented by the Five Star Movement and the Northern League respectively, then the *gilets jaunes* (yellow vests) in France, more anarchic and violent since refusing to put any sort of leader in command, even one from their own ranks, who appeared on the streets 18 months after the election of a young, centrist president. These populist movements have very similar ingredients and characteristics: so-called anti-establishment demonstrations, and the demand for an immediate, imaginary, democracy without mediation or any need to vote but with the power, nevertheless, to require the departure of leaders or the 'deselection' of elected members of Parliament.[iii]

[iii] In the United Kingdom, a member of Parliament who no longer represents the opinions of his base can be deselected by the local branch of his party.

This illusory and harmful rejection of political competence and experience makes it difficult for politicians to govern since the people have become all-powerful or, to use a word invented by the French, a *peuplecratie*.[12] It is important to draw lessons from this for our democracies and for the European Union, which remains a relevant force on the world stage, more so given the risk that populists, who have been muted during management of the COVID pandemic, may well be waiting in the wings, ready to exploit the economic inequalities and frustrations to which the pandemic has given rise.

At an internal level, the unity of the United Kingdom is under threat. The risk of Scotland seceding and Ireland reunifying is like an ever-present sword of Damocles. Scotland, which voted Remain, wanted to stay in the European Union at any cost. Brexit offers a new opportunity for a referendum on independence, more so in that relations between London and Edinburgh have deteriorated as a result of management of the health crisis. In August 2020, a YouGov poll gave 53 per cent of Scots in favour of independence the first time (a figure to be treated with caution, naturally).[13] Ireland was the stumbling block for the negotiations under Theresa May since that is where the border with the EU lies, a border which must be subject to controls in order to prevent smuggling. There were two possible options here: a land border between the North and the South, or a border in the sea between Northern Ireland and Great Britain. Theresa May declared that no British prime minister could ever accept the latter option, which did not prevent Boris Johnson from agreeing to it in October 2019 in order to conclude the deal. It did not stop him from backtracking on the issue during subsequent negotiations with the European Union either.

At an international level, Britain will need to overcome many contradictions in its dealings with other nations at a time when China, Russia, India or Turkey harbour dreams of empire under the leadership of strong men, when there is unilateralism in the United States and when global challenges are of primary importance. Britain will be forced to make choices between developing the trade links it will require by reason of its divorce from the European Union on one hand and the desire to pursue a policy founded on principles or values which risk antagonising the very countries it needs to trade with on the other. A telling illustration of these future contradictions was provided when, in February 2019, the Chinese government cancelled the Chancellor of the Exchequer's visit to Beijing to talk about a trade deal. This was in retaliation against hostile statements from the Minster of Defence who decided to send the aircraft carrier HMS *Queen Elizabeth* in order to enforce freedom of navigation in the South China Sea. The question of Hong Kong provides another perfect example in this respect – London first of all showed caution in its reaction to the adoption of the law on national security, before causing outrage in Beijing by facilitating the granting of British nationality to three million Hong Kong citizens.

A country's size, and the size of its market, count. This is particularly true with China but could well apply equally to the US. Even at the time when Donald Trump was so anxious to help Boris Johnson, detesting as he did the European Union, which he described as an enemy, and which he wished to challenge after the provisional trade deal signed in January 2020 by Washington and Beijing. The antagonism of the two capitals in relation to the G5 gives a foretaste of how much room for manoeuvre will be available to London, which has already changed its position on the subject. There is a parallel with the sentiment famously expressed by the former American Secretary of State Dean Acheson, following the failed Suez expedition: 'Great Britain has lost an empire and has not yet found a role'. The United Kingdom has lost its membership of the European Union and now has to find its role in the world.

The United Kingdom has thus chosen a solitary path, rather than one of solidarity, at a time when the world is changing. A state's power and capacity for action usually depends on its belonging to a maximum number of decision-making groups – the composition of which varies but includes UN, NATO, G20 and the EU – not by being an outside observer. Those who are not members usually try to join. It is unprecedented for those who are members to decide to leave....

The Brexit mindset, consisting of systematically taking a different position from the Europeans in the name of a mythical British exceptionalism, has even affected the fight against the COVID pandemic. At first, obsessed with putting Brexit to bed, Boris Johnson paid little attention to the looming crisis and didn't even chair the first five meetings of the UK's emergency response team, COBRA, the equivalent of France's *Conseil de Défense*.[iv] His first reflex was to refuse to use confinement to protect the population, thinking rather to create herd immunity – an option which, according to an Imperial College study, would have led to hundreds of thousands of deaths – and to believe himself invulnerable, boasting about shaking everyone's hand, which led him straight to the intensive care services of the NHS. Happily, he left hospital cured, discovering at the same time the extreme competence and dedication of the doctors and nurses, many of them of foreign origin and thus vilified by Brexiteers during the 2016 campaign. Lastly, in similar fashion, he chose to ignore a joint European order for respirators, preferring to ask Trump, who himself was short of them, and the vacuum manufacturer Dyson, a request which came to nothing. *In fine*, along with Italy, the number of deaths in the UK was the highest in Europe.

In the same way that the coronavirus pandemic destabilised Donald Trump's campaign for re-election, it interfered with the ambitions of Boris Johnson to pull off his 'fantastic Brexit' by the end of the year 2020. The mismanagement of the crisis by the two populist leaders also affected their popularity.

[iv] COBRA: Cabinet Office Briefing Room A.

The new strategic and economic context in which Brexit took place on 1 January 2021 will have particular consequences for the United Kingdom.

By revealing the relationships between different countries, the SARS-COV-2 pandemic highlighted, rather than modified, global balances of power reflecting marked trends that have been underway for some years. At the height of the storm, many thought this might well give rise to a new world order. Was that so certain? Everyone tends to see things from their own point of view and consider that their prior beliefs have been vindicated. For anti-liberals, the crisis is one of globalisation and neoliberalism, meaning that the solution is a return to a form of self-sufficiency and protectionism. Those in favour of negative growth and frugality will perhaps be less able to convince others, given that the health crisis will be followed by an economic one worse than that of 2008. For supporters of sovereignty, the solution is to close national borders; for ecologists, the crisis stems from the harm to nature caused by man – global warming, deforestation – but viruses have always existed in nature. Fatal pandemics in centuries gone by saw Pericles die from the plague in the 4th century BC and half the population of Europe succumb to the Black Death in the 14th century. Closer to our time, there was the St Petersburg 'flu', perhaps the first COVID epidemic, between 1889 and 1894, and the infamous Spanish flu just over a century ago. Or more recently still, polio in the 1940s and 1950s, Asian flu in 1957 and Hong Kong flu in 1969, the last two mentioned both having mysteriously faded from our memories.

This new pandemic is not caused by modern man exploiting nature, but on the contrary by an ancestral practice, namely the use of wild animals in traditional medicine, a practice which the young in China despair of since it gives an archaic image of their country. This is not to say that protection of the environment and biodiversity should be ignored, quite the opposite.

The pandemic has illustrated the failure of multilateralism, which was already flagging. There has been almost no international co-operation, and international institutions – notably the WHO, accused of being under Chinese influence – have been judged not fit for purpose. The UN Security Council has been invisible, confirming its powerlessness in recent years to solve any crises, or even adopt the slightest resolution.

As for the EU, even though public health is not within its remit, there is a general feeling that it did not play its role of protection and coordination in the beginning. The individual states took centre stage, which is not illegitimate when, as with military intervention, it is a question of life or death for their citizens. Borders were closed down, but there was a flagrant lack of real solidarity and the 'war of the masks' illustrated this less than glorious moment of 'every man for himself'.

This is, notwithstanding, a worldwide catastrophe of unprecedented proportions, which has seen half of humankind forced into lockdown, then plunged into an economic crisis that at one time has been compared to that of 1929. The European Union must now, in the second phase, prove its worth. This has become an existential question for the EU.

Otherwise, the European Union – or worse, its individual member states, divided – will be reduced to choosing between the two giants: Washington and Beijing.

These two powers are now facing off against each other. Some go as far as to say that it's a new type of cold war characterised notably by the uncoupling of their trading links, advocated by Trump, even though the situation is nothing like the American–Soviet stand-off, given the interdependence of the Chinese and American economies and especially China's growing share of the world economy.

Sino–American relations had not been so bad since Kissinger's visit to China in 1972. With Donald Trump declaring a trade and technological war on China, the United States really seemed to have fallen into the 'Thucydides trap',[14] described by the Greek historian in *The History of the Peloponnesian War*.[15] The paranoia of Washington in the role of Sparta, the established power, against the upcoming one, Beijing, in the role of Athens, gave rise to a virulent political conflict which could have been avoided.

The paradox was that if America's power and influence seemed to be on the decline – in spite of the perennial supremacy of the dollar ('their currency but our problem', to invert the words of John Connally, US Treasury Secretary under Nixon), its enormous military capacity (a military budget equivalent to that of all other nations) and its capacity for technological innovation – the cause was not so much China as its own president. With his campaign slogan 'America First', Donald Trump decided to pull the United States out of various theatres of operation and renounce the role of policeman of the world. This was a defensible policy choice, except that he decided at the same time to disparage his European allies, deemed harmful to the United States. Rightly or wrongly, he adopted the opposite position to the interventionist approach of the Democrats at the time when Secretary of State Madeleine Albright saw the United States, with the support of its allies, as being the 'indispensable nation' for the defence of democracy throughout the world. By taking no interest in, and disengaging from, the Middle East, the American President left the door open to Russia. Donald Trump no doubt had his acolytes in the American Rust Belt and Midwest, but in the Middle East, as in Africa, the United States had lost influence and 'soft power'. The strong leaders in charge of other big countries, who also wanted to make China or Russia great again, were more popular in their countries than was Trump. To such an extent that, in the words of an ambassador in the region, Moscow – thanks to its policy in Syria – became the new Mecca for Middle Eastern leaders, thus making it an indispensable interlocutor on the international scene. Putin had shown that, unlike American presidents, he was loyal and didn't abandon his friends.

Following the Chinese model, but using security rather than financial resources, the Russian President succeeded in organising a first Russia–Africa summit with 46 heads of state and government in October 2019. In this way, Beijing and Moscow were acquiring a large number of client states and support for their positions at the UN in direct competition with the West. Twenty years ago, the France–Africa summit was the only forum of this type involving Africa, and our candidates won the votes of Francophone African countries, while the British did the same with Anglophone ones.

Most importantly, the old empires of Russia and China, which have always distrusted each other, have been enjoying a honeymoon period, unprecedented in the last 400 years, after Russia was the first to open a foreign delegation in China. It is not an alliance as strictly defined since Beijing rejects any system of alliance. It would in any event be an uneven one inasmuch as, unlike Russia, China is a real geo-economic power, but Xi Jinping went so far as to say, using most unusual language, that Putin was his 'best friend'. The new Tsar of all Russia and the new Emperor of China understand each other well, and their interests on the international scene are similar when dealing with the West. Some in Moscow and Beijing joke that the Russians and Chinese should erect a statue of Donald Trump together, as a token of their friendship. Henry Kissinger advised the American President always to maintain better relations with each of Beijing and Moscow than the two capitals had with each other. The least that can be said is that this advice has not been followed of late. Where the two countries fought each other on the banks of the Oussouri 50 years ago, is precisely where they now choose to organise joint military manoeuvres, and their partnership is getting stronger in other strategic areas. At the United Nations, Beijing and Moscow united in their desire to block any European initiative based on human rights more than ever, as we saw in Libya, then Syria.

What has changed today, especially since Xi Jinping consolidated his power and increased his control over the population, is that China, the second world power, buoyed by its economic successes, is no longer willing to be told what to do by the West. We find it difficult to understand that what to us is the normal defence of our values and the superiority of democracy, is to the

Chinese leaders propaganda, pure and simple, and interference in their affairs. Still on the defensive at the time of Hu Jintao, they have now gone on the offensive and are more than willing to give as good as they get, inexpertly and brutally, in the case of the ultra-nationalistic and arrogant 'Wolf Warriors'. They have had no hesitation, sometimes to the chagrin of their elders, in trampling on diplomatic niceties. Simply desirous of ensuring respect for their own model of governance and development, the Chinese did not try to preach or convert anyone in the past. Is that set to change? Certainly since 2010, some people, mostly in the West, have claimed that the 'Washington Consensus' (a set of liberal rules used by the International Monetary Fund (IMF) and the World Bank for granting development aid conditional upon good governance by recipient countries) has been replaced by the 'Beijing Consensus' (development without democracy). The latter is designed to attract developing countries, especially in Africa where China is investing more and more resources. But European countries were never a target for Chinese propaganda even at the height of the Cultural Revolution when self-styled Maoist parties in Europe were looked on with profound distrust by Beijing.

Despite originating in China, the SARS-COV-2 pandemic has provided an opportunity for the Chinese. Proud of having contained the disease through the application of drastic measures, Beijing has been able to present itself as a generous and efficient supplier of epidemiologists, masks and other medical equipment to European countries, and even American ones, which were hopelessly unprepared and whose management of the situation was chaotic. While it was easy for them to point to the shortcomings of the West, the Chinese overplayed their hand by claiming that their system – characterised by discipline, a sense of community, Confucius principles and public-spiritedness – was clearly superior. In fact most of Asia – including relatively democratic societies such as South Korea, Hong Kong, Taiwan and Singapore – reasoned in a similar fashion, emphasising these same Asian values as opposed to the perceived individualism of Westerners. But unlike China, they did not link them to any particular political system.

For its part, Beijing considers that the superiority of its authoritarian regime has been proved and that these values are embodied in the Communist Party, which is totally at one with Xi Jinping's vision of China. This is in no way a Communist ideal, but a system of reinforced internal control of a Leninist variety designed to win and retain power above all else. We are very far from the Chernobyl effect predicted by the Western press at the beginning of the pandemic, since the *perestroika* (restructuring) and *glasnost* (openness) which resulted from that event were analysed in Beijing as the reason why the Soviet Union exploded and why the Communist Party disappeared. May God, Mao or the Yellow Emperor save China from such a fate! When Xi Jinping was the party's school director, the collapse of the USSR was regarded as a case study, the conclusion being that everything must be done to prevent the same thing happening in China.

On the international scene, China will no doubt continue with its vision of power and the preservation of its interests, now present in most of the world. The ambitious project of establishing new silk roads will remain at the heart of its international policy, despite the inevitable temporary hold because of the post-COVID economic crisis. The increasing involvement of Beijing in the United Nations system, which the West sees as 'entryism', will also continue. This is not illegitimate, whatever is said about it, except in the case of Interpol, when its Chinese president was recalled to Beijing in somewhat mysterious circumstances and convicted of corruption. It is a logical development for the world's second power, which for so long remained on the margins of the system monopolised by the West, and has significantly increased its contributions at the request of those same Western countries that had also regularly expressed the wish that China would take on more responsibilities.

We no longer have the monopoly of power: Europe's share is shrinking both in demographic terms and as a percentage of the volume of global Gross National Product (GNP), and therefore also in terms of influence. As the political commentator Bertrand Badie puts it so well: 'We are no longer alone in the world'.[16] In February 2020, the Annual Security Conference in Munich, known as the Davos of Defence, drew attention to this shift by choosing the decline of the West in the world as a topic – termed 'Westlessness' – but this timely analysis was quickly forgotten with the arrival of the pandemic in Europe.

Yet, we continue to see ourselves as at the centre of the world, relegating other countries to the periphery. According to World Bank and IMF forecasts, the influence of the G7 is on the wane and it will become increasingly irrelevant by the mid-2020s, when China will have become the leading world economic power with the United Kingdom and France falling to ninth and tenth, respectively, on the list of the most advanced economies. Canada and Italy will, purely and simply, disappear from this list to be replaced by India, Indonesia, Russia or Brazil. Other bodies such as BRICS (Brazil, Russia, India, China, South Africa) and, above all, the Shanghai Cooperation Organisation (SCO), which comprises the biggest Asian countries together with Russia, have been created. We do not belong to these more discreet bodies, and pay no attention to them. And while we were looking elsewhere, in November 2020 China, along with 14 countries in the region, signed the world's biggest free trade agreement representing 30 per cent of the world's population and 30 per cent of its GDP. There will, therefore, no doubt be a period of coexistence, at least in the immediate future, or indeed competition between democracies and authoritarian regimes. But are we confident of winning in emerging or developing countries? Even the countries of the European Union are divided on this point. One thing is certain – no particular political system has really emerged as the winner in this health crisis. And above all, no one is in any position to throw stones or lecture others.

The main Western powers are going to have to recover from this triple blow to health, the economy and also governance. How have these countries, so sure of themselves and of their superiority, been reduced to locking down their populations while counting their dead on a daily basis? What this pandemic has highlighted, even more clearly, is the failure of the United States and its total lack of leadership, characterised by the incoherent and extravagant declarations of Donald Trump. The trade and technological competition and conflicts between Washington and Beijing will be the key factors in the decades to come.

No one would have anything to gain from an angry confrontation, and let us not forget the extent to which economies are intertwined. There are limits to industrial repatriations, with the exception of a few strategic goods. American consumers would lose out, as would the big American companies that are installed in China, not so much because of the lower production costs since Chinese wages are increasing year on year, as for the market of one billion four hundred million consumers. General Motors sells more cars in China than in the United States, and Tesla has installed its Gigafactory for constructing electric vehicles and batteries in Shanghai. The same is true for European companies. After the war of words and the 'China bashing' which characterised the campaign of both sides in the American election, it is important to lower the temperature and revert to reason. The announcement of the implementation of a trade truce agreed in early 2020, designed to reduce the American trade deficit, was a step in this direction, following another piece of advice from Kissinger that strategic cooperation is preferable to strategic confrontation. The election of Joe Biden has not changed the general approach towards China although he will conduct himself in a more courteous manner and focus less on the tariff war which has made goods more expensive for the American consumer without reducing the trade deficit with China – quite the contrary.

France and the European Union will have to decide how to approach this question. It would be a mistake to join a particular camp on the basis of a Pavlovian reflex without taking our own interests into account. We have become accustomed to think in terms of a systematic alliance and friendship with the United States, but our interests do not automatically coincide. It is not acceptable for Washington to use extraterritorial sanctions to dictate with which countries members of the European Union may trade. NATO, American to the core, is an instrument that Washington now intends to use against China. China is no doubt a systemic rival of the United States but is it really also of Europe? It is of course a competitor and its interests, especially commercial ones, can clash with ours. We should react by ensuring that we possess all the instruments we need to defend ourselves, and we should not be afraid to use them. But let us beware of 'China bashing' that would turn a competitor into an enemy. No one would be the winner.

After the divisions and mistakes made in managing the health crisis, the European Union is returning to its core competencies: the economy and growth. Because size is all-important, the EU, as the biggest trading block in the world with its 450 million inhabitants, bestows a multiplier effect to the benefit of each member state, large or small, in their dealings with the continent-sized countries. The key here is strategic autonomy, meaning greater autonomy in terms of defence and of trade policy. Technological sovereignty is also of crucial importance. It is striking to note that during lockdown, the digital application that made it possible to continue working was Zoom, an American invention created in Silicon Valley by a Chinese man from the province of Shandong. Europe simply cannot afford to stand on the sidelines of technological innovation.

It is true that room for manoeuvre for the European Union is small, between the risks of American paranoia and Chinese hubris. But small changes to these positions are possible, in the case of America because of the wish to have the support of allies and the desire to prioritise diplomacy, and in the case of China, by the realisation that arrogance and aggression are counter-productive, giving rise as they do to unprecedented distrust of China on the part of Western nations. If it reforms itself and strengthens its solidarity and cohesion, particularly within the Eurozone, the EU might be able to play the role of mediator between the two elephants, as it did at the World Assembly of the WHO in May 2020. Things have already changed, with the formation of a recovery and assistance fund for the most vulnerable countries. Additionally, the very end of 2020 saw the signature of an agreement with Beijing on investments enabling improved access to the Chinese market and the taking into account of European concerns, despite pressure from the Americans. But the two major continent-sized countries have time on their side: the United States because of hegemonic instruments such as the dollar, and China, the only G20 country to have returned to growth in 2020, because it can continue to implement its global strategy in full without the electoral constraint of having to please public opinion.

The United Kingdom will be faced with the same dilemma as Europe, with which, like it or not, its destiny is linked. In the game of power-play, it will be difficult for it to go it alone. It will be tempted to lean towards the American position over which, however, it will have no influence. The type of relationships, economic and other, that it maintains with the European Union will be the key to its success in the post-Brexit era.

CHAPTER I

The Day Before: London, New City
of the World

RETURNING TO LONDON in the summer of 2014 from a booming China, I was astonished to find an extraordinary sense of vitality and dynamism in the city, comparable to Shanghai. A new skyline had been created, with futuristic skyscrapers in the City and beyond London Bridge. Some 200 towers were awaiting construction; in fact, the representative of Bouygues told me that there weren't enough cranes for all the work in order. There were cranes opposite Westminster and cranes looming over the gardens of Buckingham Palace, which provided an unusual backdrop for the Queen's garden parties.

Whereas 'the sky's the limit' in New York and Shanghai, in London the building frenzy stretched underground as well, towards the centre of the earth. The ground below houses could be excavated to the maximum depth possible, so 'Mega-basements' were all the rage. My neighbour in London, a former real estate developer from Foxtons Estate Agents, had submitted an enormous project involving the construction of a two-storey basement under the house and entire garden, which included a garage with a carousel lift to park his collection of vintage cars. Since this project risked weakening the foundations and proper functioning of the French Residence, successive French ambassadors – supported by their counterparts residing in the very chic, leafy Kensington Palace Gardens – challenged it before the courts. The press reported on the case with articles criticising such megalomaniac projects that were springing up all over London. One day, an entire Georgian house collapsed. The neighbours, intent on digging giant

underground galleries beneath their own houses, complained bitterly about the endless noise and dust.

Jonathan Coe – whose novels deal with contemporary English
history, including its quirks and whims – chose this subject as the
theme of his book, *Number 11*.[1] Although this number refers to
the chancellor of the exchequer's residence at 11 Downing Street,
it so happens that the address of the French Residence is number
11 Kensington Palace Gardens. So, when awarding this talented
writer a medal for his services to the arts, I was able to open my
speech with: 'Welcome to number eleven, dear Jonathan Coe.'

London, a sad and grey city in the '70s, rose more than once
from its ashes, resplendent and self-confident in the 2010s. The
Olympic Games of 2012 – a veritable apotheosis that saw the
'Queen' parachute jump into the Olympic stadium opening ceremony with James Bond – elicited euphoria and optimism. This
symbolic sequence demonstrated the British *savoir-faire* and
ever-present sense of humour, its success foreshadowing the record
medal haul at the end of the Games. They were 'the 15 best days
of my life' a young British journalist told me, and I know that
such jubilation and pride were feelings widely shared.

Now, London appeared as the new cosmopolitan city of the
world, a serious rival to New York. The success of the urban
planning project for the Queen Elizabeth Olympic Park in
Stratford mirrored the redevelopment of East London, a place
that no longer resembled the slums described by Louis-Fer-
dinand Céline in *Guignol's Band*. Bold architectural projects
abounded, such as the new Tate Modern (the opening of which
I attended in 2016) or the Serpentine Gallery in Kensington
Gardens, designed by the highly talented and creative Anglo–
Iraqi architect, Zaha Hadid, whose offices just so happened to
be in London.

There was always something going on in London. Like Paris,
London is its country's political, economic, scientific and cultural capital all in one. Living on Greenwich Mean Time meant
that it was possible to communicate with both the East and West

without too much of a time difference. Many Americans, Asians and entrepreneurs from the Middle East had chosen to set up the headquarters of their businesses there; at 3.1 per cent at the beginning of the 2000s, growth was the highest in Europe and in the G7. Unemployment was very low and confined to full-time work even though many jobs were precarious, notably those involving zero-hour contracts. This often meant that those concerned were obliged to find a second, equally precarious, job; however, this arrangement suited many students or those with significant family constraints, allowing them to maintain a continuous link with the job market.

In 2012 Boris Johnson, the then charismatic and provocative mayor of London, said he was ready to roll out the red carpet for French investors dismayed by a 75 per cent tax rate, the rigidity of the labour market and the complexity of the process required to set up a company in France. Parliamentary and institutional delegations, right up to Prime Minister Manuel Valls and the Minister for the Economy Emmanuel Macron, crossed the Channel in search of the recipe for growth and optimism. There were several special editions on London published in the French press at the time. Boris Johnson later took pride in telling me (incorrectly) that he was mayor of the fourth-largest French city, with a population of some 250,000 French nationals. He even boasted to Alain Juppé, then mayor of Bordeaux, that he administered a French city bigger than his.

The French were a varied community, ranging from mathematicians, former students of French polytechnic schools, and City financiers (the Head of the London Stock Exchange for ten years was a highly respected Frenchman, Xavier Rollet). There were the French chefs and waiters in the best restaurants or bistros; French engineers; stage directors and artistes such as Sylvie Guillem, or Julien Clerc; and a dynamic business community in which all sectors of activity were represented. There was even a radio station, French Radio London, which broadcast exclusively in French. With no culture of economic patriotism at the time, the consumer's interest alone prevailed, and large French companies had won contracts for the provision of electricity (EDF), waste and water management (Veolia) and transport services. The logo of the French RATP (*Régie Autonome des Transports Parisiens*) was clearly visible on the iconic red buses of London managing, as it did, several of their routes. French start-ups joined CAC40 companies to create a dynamic 'French tech', bringing the total number of French companies implanted in the UK to around 3,000. (On a visit to Scotland, I was astonished to discover that the principal whisky brands were under French ownership.) Young people arrived from the French suburbs, sure of finding work; the Charles Péguy centre, a French charity, helped them integrate socially and professionally.

There really was, and still is, a French town in London, organised around its schools – particularly the 100-year-old first among them, Charles-de-Gaulle, located in the French Quarter in South Kensington, with the Institute and its cinema Lumière, bookshops, cafes and bakeries. French could be heard everywhere in the surrounding streets; a young French schoolboy, long before the Brexit campaign, even wrote to the local council to request a referendum on whether South Kensington should become independent in order to take account of its special nature. Given the rapid expansion of the French community, and in order to preserve the link with our culture for future generations, we opened two further schools: the first in Kentish Town, then another in Wembley in the former Brent town hall (in the most multicultural quarter of London). In 2016, we named this school after Winston Churchill in the presence of his grandson and the French President. It was extremely rare for a French school abroad to be given the name of someone who was not French, and this was in gratitude for the welcome accorded General de Gaulle and the Free French Forces during the war. Several British people confided that they were pleased to see the opening of new French schools and their attendant 'civilised' ecosystem – meaning baguettes and croissants!

But in spite of our high visibility, we were far from being the biggest foreign community; in fact, we only came tenth. We were greatly outnumbered by Indians, Pakistanis, Germans, Greeks, Cypriots and Poles as well as many others, varying in number, for example Sudanese, Eritreans and Nigerians – all the Commonwealth. Each community had its own restaurants, food shops and sometimes hospitals, like the Cromwell Hospital financed by the Emirates where, fleeing the searing summer heat of the Gulf, men in dishdashas and women in niqabs could be seen. Some communities had their own newspaper, radio and television programmes or television series devoted to them.

The British capital was already a city of the world in the sense that 40 per cent of its inhabitants were born abroad. Almost every nationality in the world is represented in London today, and more than 200 languages are spoken, making it no doubt the most cosmopolitan city on the planet. Some areas have indeed been baptised accordingly: Chinatown, Little India, Londongrad, or Londonistan (of sinister reputation). The area around Finsbury Mosque is even nicknamed 'The Islamic Republic of Tower Hamlets'; Londoha, is so named because of the number of purchases made by Qatar. Qatar and its businessmen own two of the tallest towers in London (one being the Shard), the luxury store Harrods, the Olympic village and the new business quarter Canary Wharf, where more than 100,000 people work and where the big international banks have set up their headquarters. All the world's festivals, from the Chinese New Year with its dragons and lions to the Indian Diwali festival of lights, are celebrated in the city. London has therefore become a real gastronomic centre in which all the cuisines of the world can be found, cooked by Michelin-starred chefs, in some cases.

The Chinese community no longer lives in Chinatown in Soho, one of the oldest Chinese quarters in the world which has today become, rather, an area of restaurants. The community is dispersed and diverse, comprising of Chinese from the continent, people from Taiwan, and Hong Kong tycoons such as the delightful David Tang, founder of the Shanghai Tang brand and boutiques and columnist in the *Financial Times*, arbiter of good taste and the art of living well. He generously used to invite his friends to the Chinese New Year festivities and to sumptuous dinners which brought together intellectuals, artists, businessmen and politicians of all persuasions – from Tony Blair to Monica Lewinsky. I even saw Nigel Farage there once, to the great astonishment and displeasure of the other guests of note. I got on well with David Tang because I was posted to Hong Kong at the beginning of my career. He was an eccentric who had panache, just as they like them in London, and a big heart. Diagnosed with cancer, he wrote to all his friends during the summer of 2017 to inform them that the 'political bureau' of his doctors only gave him a month or two to live and that he wanted to throw a big goodbye party on the 6th September. Unfortunately, he died before then which is extremely sad, even though the 'party' would have been incredibly gloomy.

The Chinese, with Geely, have invested in London's iconic black cabs and become interested in the reconstruction of the Crystal Palace where Britain, at the height of its imperial glory, welcomed visitors to the Universal Exhibition. The new nuclear power station at Hinkley Point is being built by EDF and the China General Nuclear Power Group (CGN) and it was decided that the next EPR (Evolutionary Power Reactor) would make use of Chinese technology. Everyone is present in London, even the Falun Gong movement, banned in China, which demonstrates permanently in front of the Chinese Embassy and in Chinatown.

On a state visit in October 2015, President of China Xi Jinping described London as being China's gateway to Europe and announced the beginning of a golden decade for relations between the two countries. In the most important speech of his visit, given in Guildhall in the heart of the City, he paid homage to the oldest democracy in the world. The biggest Chinese investment fund Ginkgo Tree, with its immense Chinese reserves, had chosen the British capital as the centre from which to engage with the rest of the European Union. The infatuation with London amongst the Chinese at the time of this visit was so strong that several weeks later, when I was in Beijing myself, I saw red buses and telephone boxes in the chic quarter of Sanlitun, in front of which fashionable young Pekinese were taking photographs of each other.

Some communities in London, because of their historical links, have also become involved in politics. For example, the Indian community are represented in Westminster by Lords and members of Parliament who meet in 'curry clubs' and various friendship groups, not to mention the influential British–India All Parliamentary Association. Priti Patel, a virulent Brexiteer, was for a while a minister in Theresa May's government and is now home secretary in Boris Johnson's. A favourite amongst the Tories in today's Cabinet is the Chancellor of the Exchequer Rishi Sunak, whose family is originally from the Punjab.

Several British citizens of Pakistani origin have made a brilliant career in all branches of politics, including Sajid Jawid, who has been a Conservative minister several times, and the Mayor of London Sadiq Khan, both sons of bus drivers and proud of their success. The election of a Muslim head of a major Western metropolis in May 2016, while regarded almost as a non-event in the capital of the United Kingdom, was a much-talked-about subject in France and gave rise to a plethora of requests for meetings from French local or national celebrities passing through London. Keen to represent all communities, including those from the European Union, Sadiq Khan takes every opportunity to proclaim that London is, and will remain, open to all. He invited me, together with the ambassadors of other significant communities, to the City Hall immediately after Brexit in order to transmit this message.

* * *

Since the 1990s, with the arrival of oligarchs attracted by low taxes for the expatriate rich and golden visas, the Russian community in London has been growing. Londongrad or 'Moscow-on-Thames' went from strength to strength and the population increased from just about 15,000 at the beginning of the 21st century to roughly 300,000 today. Super-rich and influential oligarchs have become owners of football clubs – Chelsea was bought by Roman Abramovitch, for example – or of newspapers, like Alexander Lebedev who bought *The Independent* and then the very influential London daily, the *Evening Standard*. Opposition figures such as Mikhail Khodorkovsky, the former boss of the private oil company Yukos, which was nationalised by the Kremlin, live side by side. In the grand tradition of things, each have spies and double agents. The latest illustration was the fateful case of the attempted poisoning of a former double agent, Sergei Skripal, and his daughter with Novichok in March 2018 in Salisbury, not far from London, ten years after the assassination of Litvinenko using Polonium. After the intervention in Ukraine and the fall of the rouble, 90 per cent of the capital fleeing Russia sought refuge in London; The book *Londongrad, From Russia with Cash* gives an account of this new immigration.[2] Because of it, the British capital became the most expensive real estate on the planet. The anti-corruption company ClampK, founded by Roman Borisovitch, organises 'Klepto Tours' of luxurious London properties bought with 'dirty' money.

The Russian presence was also tangible in the city's culture: the bookshop chain Waterstones, struggling financially, was purchased and turned around by Alexander Mamut. Dmitri Khvorostovsky, the unforgettable baritone with snow-white hair, sang *Eugene Onegin* at the Royal Opera House Covent Garden while Valery Gergiev conducted the London Symphony Orchestra for a while. It is interesting to note that Helen Mirren, made a Dame by Her Majesty whom she played to perfection in the film *The Queen,* was born Ilynea Lydia Mironoff, her father being a member of the Russian military aristocracy. Mirren played the role of the Queen once more, on stage in the play *The Audience* by Peter Morgan. The subject of this play was the weekly audiences the Queen holds with her prime ministers, from Winston Churchill to David Cameron, and it was a marvel of intelligence, humour and veracity. The last act was modified in order to reflect the latest news; an actor had begun to rehearse the role of Ed Miliband in anticipation of the general election of 2015, but the scene portrayed the triumphant return of David Cameron instead. Unfortunately, the play had finished running before the arrival of Theresa May. One day, perhaps, it will return, when the Brexit epilogue is known....

Above all, London has become a European city, counting more than three million inhabitants who came from the continent and who, immediately after the referendum, opened a Twitter account called 'the3million' and drafted petitions concerning protection of the rights of EU citizens living in the UK. All of them, with the exception of the one million or so Irish, were denied the vote – even those who had lived in London for more than 20 years.

At nearly one million members, the Polish community was the largest of the Europeans. After the enlargement of the EU, they were attracted by the enthusiastic welcome and job prospects in the United Kingdom, when France declared it didn't want to see 'Polish plumbers arriving'. In fact, it was Polish workers, who could be seen and heard every morning arriving on building sites, who built the new London and the Olympic park. Many Romanians arrived subsequently, and one-sixth of the Lithuanian population emigrated to London. They were a young and dynamic population and, contrary to what Brexiteers claimed, made little use of social services, in which many of them worked.

A veritable cosmopolitan city, then, but a mosaic in which people often cross paths without actually meeting. The much-vaunted multiculturalism claimed as a model in comparison to the French policy of integration, has also failed. David Cameron admitted as much, and Tony Blair himself recognised that the enemies of liberty could not be allowed to abuse this same liberty. Louise Casey, in charge of welfare inspection, published a remarkable report on integration in the United Kingdom revealing abuses, notably in relation to the case of the gang rape and exploitation of young girls by members of the Pakistani community in Rother-ham. But, it received only a cautious imprimatur in 2016, such was the sensitivity of the subject and the strength of the myth of happy multiculturalism. For his part, Michael Wilshaw, a former head of OFSTED, the education inspectorate, reported some wor-rying facts and highlighted the dangers of a policy that consisted of closing your eyes. (I have had some fascinating meetings with him and with Louise Casey.) The proportion of those who went to wage jihad in Syria was, in fact, the same as in France. The most cruel and bloodthirsty representatives were the four terror-ists – nicknamed 'the Beatles' by their hostages because of their English accents – including Jihadi John, who could be seen on videos decapitating captives of Daesh which, for months, were headline news.

I pointed out this fact when, after the *Charlie Hebdo* attacks, some of the British media chose to blame them on the 'aggressive secularism' practised by France. The Bataclan and Nice attacks, which elicited immense sympathy and solidarity, attenuated these criticisms somewhat. Later, in 2017, the Islamist terrorist attacks at Westminster and on London Bridge, in which the French com-munity paid a heavy price with three dead and several wounded, and then in Manchester resulting in 22 deaths at a concert for teenagers and children, shook these convictions. However, even though a policy to combat radicalisation has been pursued, this has not led to a genuine reflection about, or questioning of, mul-ticulturalism. Some years later, all that seemed forgotten when the British press blamed the decapitation of the teacher Mr Paty in France on those who had shown the *Charlie Hebdo* cartoons. The policy of radical multiculturalism had even tolerated Sharia courts in which an imam judges family matters not, according to some testimonies, to the benefit of women.

Over and above the people making up the city's population, London was the world capital of finance, insurance, law and infor-mation. The City of London was known, first and foremost, as the headquarters of world finance, its population as multicultural as that of the rest of the capital with more than 40 per cent foreign passport holders. The City, famous for its bowler-hatted bankers and enjoying worldwide prestige, is an entity *sui generis*. Once past the dragon statues that guard the borders of the territory, we enter into the Square Mile administered by the Lord Mayor and inducted with great ceremony every year with a parade of the principal guilds dressed in medieval costume – even the Queen has to ask permission in order to enter. The City has its own administration and police. It is said that Jack the Ripper was never caught due to a lack of communication between the forces since he took refuge in the City after having committed his crimes in the neighbouring quarter of Whitechapel.

At the end of my mandate in London and at a traditional ceremony I had the honour of receiving my diploma of 'Freeman of the City' giving me the right, amongst others, to drive my sheep over the bridge without charge. A mixture of medieval tradition and all-powerful finance, the City, upon which two million people depended for a living, ensured that its interests were defended by dispatching a representative to Brussels. In 2016, the April Fool's joke that made many laugh a few weeks before the referendum was that secret meetings were being held at night in a crypt to prepare the City's independence in the event of Brexit.

As a result of this financial power, London was also able to establish itself as the capital of insurance with the famous Lloyds, the capital of law (notably commercial law), and the world capital of arbitration. Many internal disputes between Chinese companies, or between Russian ones, were brought before a tribunal in London.

London is also the undisputed capital of information. The *Financial Times*, two-thirds of whose readers live outside the United Kingdom, instils liberal values and educates minds in Brussels, Tokyo, Shanghai and Delhi. Its readers form their view of Europe and of the world by reading the pink pages of the newspaper – the same colour has been adopted by financial pages or newspapers in other countries including *Le Figaro* in Paris and

Vedomosti in Moscow. The weekly paper, *The Economist* is read by the same elites throughout the world. The BBC, or 'Beebs', also known affectionately as 'Auntie', which often arouses the ire of Conservative governments, continues to enjoy worldwide prestige and remains the undisputed reference for all the radio and television companies of the world. It is to the BBC that China turned to train its journalists in a post-Maoist mode of information. Since 2005, Al Jazeera has broadcast in Arabic from London; Bloomberg and CNN with its star journalist Christiane Amanpour broadcast to Europe, the Middle East and Africa from London. The big agencies are dynamic, and in addition to Reuters, the Agence France-Presse (AFP) has its biggest office there from which it broadcasts in French and also in English to Europe, the Middle East and Africa. I had the sad privilege of visiting their premises as they were beginning to broadcast the news and images of the *Charlie Hebdo* killings.

The British are also masters of what they call 'talk business' – the discussion of ideas. Numerous, prestigious think tanks are based in London, the oldest being the Royal United Services Institute (RUSI). It debates issues of security and defence and was founded in 1831 by the Duke of Wellington; its honorary president is always appointed from among his descendants. Another very famous one, the Royal Institute for International Affairs based in Chatham House, has written in stone the rules of the game that apply to their equivalents throughout the world, including China and Russia. The famous Chatham House Rule is that sources of information are not disclosed, thereby allowing free debate. This reflects the activities of the debating societies in schools and universities and makes an important contribution to British soft power. The professionalism of those trained in this system is so widely recognised that when I was serving in Beijing, the mediators of roundtable discussions, even those on the euro crisis, were almost always British. Even several think tanks dealing with European issues were based in London, including the EFR of Charles Grand, or the European Council on Foreign Relations

(ECFR), founded and directed by Marc Leonard, a former adviser to Tony Blair, who felt that it didn't make sense to stay in London after Brexit, choosing to relocate to Berlin instead. Foundations such as Ditchley and Wilton Park host two-day seminars in 'heavenly' grand houses in the English countryside dotted with sheep. This makes it possible to prolong discussions, create networks and influence ideas more than in a one-day seminar in a think tank, no matter the quality of the participants.

Academic life is intense in the golden triangle comprising the big London universities of Imperial College London, University College London, and the London School of Economics and Political Science, and the two prestigious university towns of Oxford and Cambridge which are models for all the Ivy League universities in the English-speaking world and beyond. They of course also score very highly on all international rankings, including Shanghai. The Chinese tourists who come to shop at the sales in Selfridges, Harvey Nichols and Harrods also go to see the mythical 'Platform 9 ¾' at King's Cross and never fail to visit the large medieval refectories of the colleges, or the superb Bodleian library at Oxford which was used in the filming of *Harry Potter*. JK Rowling rekindled the desire to read in millions of children throughout the world, all looking at things through the eyes of a young English boy, of course a sympathetic wizard, but English all the same. Soft power in all its glory!

These establishments are attended by a large number of non-natives, from Europe and elsewhere. Chinese students often account for up to 25 per cent of these; many Chinese parents enrol their children, at the age of 13, in exclusive boarding schools such as Eton, which has educated many ministers and other famous ex-pupils: the economist John Maynard Keynes; the writers George Orwell and Ian Fleming, author of the *James Bond* books; Prince William, the future monarch; and 19 British prime ministers. Being associated with these top universities for research projects also guaranteed access to European funds.

As a result of such privileged schooling, the British political system and those working in it were considered to be models of representative democracy. Educated in excellent schools and universities, having had experience in the private sector and the world of communications, David Cameron and his Chancellor of the Exchequer George Osborne, the designated successor, incarnated a type of modern Conservatism – compassionate, and liberal in both economic and social, or societal, terms. A centrist vision shared by Nick Clegg who, until 2015, held the post of deputy prime minister created for him after the Liberal Democrat success at the 2010 general election. Foreign Secretary Philip Hammond, the former defence secretary, who would become chancellor of the exchequer in Theresa May's Cabinet, appeared as one of the most competent officials, and a sage, whose position on Europe had, thanks to his functions, evolved on the basis of objective facts. It was always a pleasure to work with him, more so in that he possessed the dry humour that is characteristic of the English. He regularly attended the 14 July reception at the French Residence and delivered part of his speech in excellent French.

In September 2015 in Manchester, at his last Conservative Party Conference – a highlight of the British political calendar – David Cameron appeared at the height of his glory having emerged victorious from the Scottish referendum and the general election (he also spoke of his pride in having succeeded in enacting a law on gay marriage). Everything seemed to be going his way: he had met his first challenge of maintaining Scotland in the union for all that the campaign had been organised in a somewhat cavalier fashion, accepting all the Scottish conditions (the right to vote from 16 years of age, electorate limited to residents of Scotland, even those recently arrived). It's true there was a last-minute panic when, for the first time, a poll gave a majority in favour of independence. This prompted David Cameron himself to call on businessmen to explain publicly what the people of an independent Scotland stood to lose in terms of purchasing power. He also persuaded the Queen, who by constitutional tradition remains silent in such circumstances, to imply her support for maintaining Scotland in the union when she called on people to 'think carefully before voting' – a good example of British understatement.

David Cameron achieved the same insolent success in the general election of 2015, despite the fact that a Labour victory – Ed Miliband's shortcomings notwithstanding – could not be totally written off, and all the experts were busy explaining the different 'hung Parliament' scenarios and the possible coalitions. The Tory Party emerged as sole victors which, without a doubt, encouraged a degree of hubris in David Cameron. He couldn't have imagined at the time that this would turn out to be a Pyrrhic victory. The ministers serving in this second mandate (like Theresa May, the respected 'safe pair of hands' appointed as home secretary) appeared to be reliable and competent. Then there was a charismatic, somewhat scruffy, mayor of London who rode around on a bicycle and made Londoners laugh with his witty remarks, peppered with phrases in Greek or Latin. Boris Johnson was the only politician known by his first name, which became a sort of brand, with 'Boris buses' or 'Boris bikes'.

David Cameron's dynamic and convincing Manchester speech promoted a veritable project. The members of this Notting Hill elite had no doubt that they would be in power for ten years, especially after the election of Jeremy Corbyn as leader of the Labour Party – a sort of Trotskyist whose policies were rooted in the 1970s. The Tories radiated assurance and self-confidence; books and various souvenirs were being sold in the conference hall – mugs showing the image of the symbolic figurehead of the Conservative Party Margaret Thatcher ('our Maggie') and bearing François Mitterrand's famous comment: 'the eyes of Caligula and the mouth of Marilyn Monroe'. Among the items for sale was David Cameron's biography *Call Me Dave*: laid-back, cool – like a sort of reincarnation of the 'Cool Britannia' of Tony Blair's glory years.[3]

These party conferences are fascinating events for the ambassadors invited since they provide the opportunity to drink in the atmosphere and talk to everybody over two days. They begin in the morning as the attendees sit down together to the *nec plus ultra* of English breakfasts: eggs, bacon, sausages, slices of black pudding, tomatoes, beans, all washed down with milky tea. During the day and in the evening we are also able to attend dozens of side events discussing hot topics of the day. For the Conservatives that year it was Brexit, while a few days earlier at the Labour Party Conference the favoured topic was Palestine. There are many representatives of civil society in attendance but these gatherings are designed for the party faithful, the most dedicated militants. Strangely, when addressing these militant supporters, party leaders sometimes seem to forget that there are foreigners present, as well as journalists.

Today, all that is forgotten and David Cameron will forever remain as the person responsible for Brexit, something that the convinced Europeans in the Conservative Party, and a good proportion of the population, continue to hold against him.

* * *

The Queen and the royal family – whose marriages, births and other events are followed with intense interest the world over – are an asset and a key element of Britain's soft power. Not many British are fervent or militant republicans, although I have met some in university circles who refuse to sing *God Save the Queen*. In any event, there seems to be a universal respect. A separatist Welsh republican one day referred to the Queen as 'Mrs Windsor', for which he was roundly criticised from within his own ranks. We were told that some Brexiteers, campaigning in a factory for the UK to leave the EU, claimed that the latter was planning to abolish the monarchy. Her Majesty is venerated and everyone who meets her agrees that audiences with her are extremely pleasant occasions.

I was able to verify this for myself at various traditional gatherings throughout the year: the garden party in the spring, or the diplomatic ball in December when she took the trouble to speak to each of her guests. And, in particular, when I spoke with her one-on-one while presenting my letters of credence before introducing four members of my team. The protocol is unchanging and solemn: crossing London in an open carriage (with a heated blanket when, as for me, the ceremony takes place at the end of autumn, or in winter); the once-in-a-lifetime passing under Wellington Arch closed to traffic and arriving, in my case, in the court of Buckingham Palace during the Changing of the Guard in their bearskin hats. Ringing at the double doors and waiting to be admitted; a first step with the left foot alongside the Marshal of the Diplomatic Corps in his imposing uniform, feathered hat and sword at his side. A first bow of the head; the Marshal withdraws. The door closes and one walks forward towards the Queen – towards history. Fascination and respect for the woman who has conversed with Churchill and de Gaulle, President Kennedy, Gandhi, Mikhail Gorbachev, Deng Xiaoping, Nelson Mandela and so many others. Our meeting was after her state visit to France for the anniversary of the Normandy landings, and she relayed how much she appreciated this visit and the memory of the Normans shouting 'Vive le duc', and even 'Vive notre duc' as she passed.

This same sentiment is shared by any British citizen who, because of their functions or merits, has had an audience with the Queen. My induction ceremony was followed by a reception at the French Residence to which the Marshal of the Diplomatic Corps escorted me. After giving carrots to the horses that pulled the royal carriage, the small reception ends with a toast to the Queen and to the President of the Republic. When I remarked to the Marshal that this was a once-in-a-lifetime moment, he jokingly asked me if one could say 'Thank You for This Moment', knowing that that very day, the English version of Valerie Trierweiler's book (of which this was the title) was being launched in a bookshop in Piccadilly.

No one knows if the successor to Queen Elizabeth will be the object of the same veneration. Prince Charles has engendered some dislike, even if the British have been reconciled with Camilla and the case of Diana, the 'People's Princess', is long ago now.

But the blameworthy image of Prince Charles as portrayed in the series *The Crown* has given rise to renewed and virulent attacks that were significant enough to warrant disabling the comments section of his Twitter account. The saga of the Prince of Wales' letters exemplifies this distrust; the heir to the throne was constantly accused of interfering in political matters by *The Guardian* which demanded publication of his letters to different members of the Government. These letters were given a somewhat sinister name, reminiscent of Agatha Christie: 'black spider memos' because of the very black ink he used and his distinctive style of writing.[4] Authorisation, at first refused by the Attorney General in 2012, was finally given by the Supreme Court in 2015; however, the affair fizzled out since Charles wrote principally about matters relating to the welfare of soldiers, architecture, agriculture and the environment – his favourite subjects. The fact is that he was a trailblazer on these issues. I had the opportunity to be invited to Clarence House, the residence of the Prince of Wales, where I was served refined tea in cups of fine porcelain. The Prince, who attended the opening of COP21, had always been active in respect of climate change issues. In 2017, I had the privilege and the pleasure of presenting him with the badge of agricultural merit, the famous green leek, on behalf of the French Minister of Agriculture. He was genuinely pleased, and indeed wore it when he met President Macron on 18 June 2020.

The system of the UK is dual in nature with a monarch who personifies the nation but has no political power. As Marc Roche pointed out, Queen Elizabeth really only governs swans, whales and sturgeons, all three of which belong to the monarch[5] – beware anyone who harms the elegant, long-necked swans in London's parks. Did she regret her discreet incursion into politics on the occasion of the Scottish referendum in order to preserve the unity of her kingdom? In any case, she clearly did not appreciate David Cameron's comment that she purred with pleasure upon hearing the result, with reference being made to her great-great-grandmother Queen Victoria's famous declaration, 'We are not amused.'

(The custom normally followed is that nothing should be said about private conversations with the Queen.) The sober and reassuring speech she gave that lasted several minutes during the first week of the pandemic was followed by a special, lengthy BBC broadcast that included many comments, lyrical in their praise. Tradition and pageantry are the prerogatives of the monarch and the royal family; it is the prime minister who governs. He (or she) lives in an unassuming bourgeois house where those visiting the civil servants whose offices are in the same building may well cross paths with the prime minister returning from jogging or his wife coming back from a shopping expedition. Doubts are increasingly expressed surrounding the relevance of the monarchy in modern times. To the question, 'What purpose does a King or a Queen serve?' is the edifying reply given by one subject of Her Majesty: 'To make sure the prime minister does not assume the mantel of monarch.'

Everything seemed to be going well in the years before Brexit. But that was London, vibrant London, where modern creativity coexisted with traditional charm. An island in the middle of an island; London and the English desert, as was said about Paris. *Paris and the French Desert* is the famous title of a book written by a geographer in the 1940s,[6] although modern regional metropolises were gradually going to develop in France.

For many, the rest of the country remained invisible and inaudible beyond the M25 – the autoroute around London, the orbital city. Chancellor of the Exchequer George Osborne did, in fact, launch the idea of a 'Northern powerhouse' designed to revitalise run-down regions and towns of the North, many of which were disfigured and sad, where majestic town halls alone bore witness to once-booming industry that sent ships from Manchester and Liverpool across the world. The economic and financial crisis of 2008 left deep scars, not only in terms of economic austerity but also of having been misled and abandoned by bankers and politicians from the City and Westminster. The differences between regions and the social inequalities, reflected in the films of Ken

Loach, were more marked than in France. According to Eurostat statistics, nine out of the ten poorest regions in Northern Europe were British.

I made sure to travel outside of London also, but I concentrated on university towns and the larger cities such as Birmingham (the world's workshop during the Industrial Revolution), Manchester, Liverpool, Cardiff and also the Scottish cities of Edinburgh and Glasgow, where the leaders I met, often Labour supporters, were in favour of remaining in the European Union and determined to campaign to that effect. These municipal leaders were, in fact, fairly confident about the outcome of the vote; however, once when I was in Portsmouth to attend the 30th anniversary of the Ouistreham–Portsmouth line run by Brittany Ferries, I was surprised to meet supporters of the Leave campaign. I remember the congenial but pugnacious station master who joked with our small delegation on the platform and continued, as the train started to move, to wave his little flag shouting 'Brexit! Brexit! Brexit!'

The former trade union leader Lord Monks returned from a visit to provincial England towards the end of the campaign and relayed what he had heard there, confessing his pessimism. Who, in London, listened to him? The truth is that the Conservatives no longer had many sensors in these regions and Labour, which had been made responsible for the campaign, had not yet realised that their leader was himself a Brexiteer. The faint signals were understood to have been meaningful afterwards – too late. The result of the referendum, announced in the early morning of 24 June 2016, appeared, therefore, like a bolt out of the blue. Nobody, or next to nobody, in the United Kingdom had seen it coming.

CHAPTER 2

An Island Nation: British Exceptionalism

This fortress built by Nature for herself,
Against infection and the hand of war,
This happy breed of men, this little world,
This precious stone set in the silver sea,
Which serves it in the office of a wall,
Or as a moat defensive to a house,
Against the envy of less happier lands,
This blessed plot, this earth, this realm, this England.

William Shakespeare

'GREAT BRITAIN IS an island surrounded on all sides by water, and I could stop there.' This was the ritual beginning to the lecture given between the wars by André Siegfried, professor at the Parisian *Ecole Libre des Sciences Politiques* – now known as *Sciences Po*. Seigfried paraphrased Jules Michelet at the *Collège de France* who said 'England is an island, and now you know as much about its history as I do.' This is where the geographer and the historian come together. 'This precious stone set in the silver sea' is a quote from Shakespeare's *Richard II*[1] that almost all British schoolchildren learn by heart, and the reference to a fortress built by nature that is supposed to protect against infection and war has a particular resonance in these times of a pandemic. In a similar tone, and indicative of this insular, 'little world' mindset, *The Times* published an article in 1957, entitled: 'Heavy Fog in the Channel. Continent cut off'.[2] Psychoanalysts recognise the importance of the family story, the one we invent, often in good faith, to make sense of our own personal history.

66

States also construct their national story – the narrative that makes sense of the present and forms the basis for future policy choices. History is written by the victors, as they say, but it is also recounted by those who feel aggrieved or frustrated in order to justify a change of direction; therefore the national narrative evolves over time.

It is amusing to note that immediately after the referendum British leaders, from Boris Johnson to Theresa May, took care to specify on several occasions that although they were leaving the European Union, they were not leaving Europe. This statement has always left me perplexed. Do they imagine they have the power to withdraw from geography, or from the history, admittedly tumultuous, that has linked Great Britain to the European continent for centuries? To form a continent on its own, or to drift westwards over the Atlantic to attach itself to the United States?

There were many seminars organised in the weeks following the shock of Brexit, in an effort to make sense of what had happened. I was often invited to attend, and I was eager to try to understand what the UK itself was having such difficulty comprehending. One of the participants assured us that all would be made clear by reading *Our Island Story*[3] – a book for children and adolescents first published in 1905. Note, 'Story', not 'History'; a story in the sense of a myth or fairy tale and not history as founded on facts, albeit open to varying interpretation. (It is indeed a romantic, glorious tale.) David Cameron said, at the time of his first election victory in 2010, that it was his favourite book as a child because it 'captured the imagination'. It is likely that he is not the only one to think of his country in this way.

For Brexiteers, the implicit narrative at the time of Brexit was, of course, one of a glorious past: an imperial nation, an empire on which the sun never set, England ruling the waves and a quarter of the earth. 'Rule Britannia! Britannia rule the waves!'.[i] The Brexiteers thought that the modern-day equivalent could be the Commonwealth – 53 member countries with the Queen at the centre, formally the head of state in 14 of them (13 following the decision of Barbados to become a republic in November 2021). The Commonwealth was supposed to provide better trading opportunities than the European Union. It seems not to occur to Brexiteers that Australia and New Zealand today lean more towards China, or Canada to the United States. Or that India, now close behind its former colonial power and on track to overtake it in the near future, feels totally independent and often irritated by the pretensions of London. Reference is also increasingly made to another concept, that of an 'Anglosphere', where everything is supposed to orbit around England, yet Washington, not London, would be the centre – surely more of an American sphere than Anglosphere then? What's more, all these countries are interested in the European market and have negotiated free trade agreements with Brussels, or are in the process of doing so. All the talk of the independence that Brexit is supposed to procure thus seems rather illusory.

UK history, as recounted by the partisans of Brexit, is also that of an ever-victorious country which has never been invaded (at least not since 1066, the date of the Norman conquest). This thanks to the dignity and stoicism exhibited by King George VI and Queen Elizabeth; the determination of Churchill; the bravery of the Royal Air Force pilots; the everyday courage of the people of London subjected to German bombing (the famous Blitz spirit); and perhaps because it is an island 'surrounded on all sides by water'. A country that thinks it won the Second World War single-handedly and liberated the continent. Where

---

[i] Patriotic song dating from 1740, often sung by supporters of the England football team: 'Rule Britannia! Britannia rule the waves! [...] The nations not so blest as thee/Must, in their turn, to tyrants fall/While thou shalt flourish great and free/The dread and envy of them all'.

does this leave the role of the Americans and the Red Army? Thanks to Hollywood, mention is sometimes made of a soldier called Ryan but never of the price paid in blood by 22 million Soviets. This, however, does nothing to dissuade Brexiteers from repeating over and over that the United Kingdom alone liberated Europe; therefore, it needs no one. A well-known cartoon from 1940 of a man saying 'Very Well, Alone'[4] after the defeat of the French army is again in circulation today, as if the two situations were comparable. In 1940 it was Hitler who isolated the British; today with Brexit they are doing it all by themselves. I certainly do not wish to minimise the role played by our British allies in liberating France and we can never thank enough those who came to our shores willing to make the supreme sacrifice, or those for whom the sun will never rise again – 'Lest we forget', as the hallowed expression goes. I simply wish to point out that they were not alone. We cannot continue to live in accordance with events that ended in 1945.

Two wonderful historical films, which proved very popular in these post-Brexit years, bear witness to the glorification of this heroic spirit. The first is *Dunkirk*, directed by Christopher Nolan in 2017, which tells the story of how an armada of small, private boats crossed the Channel to come to the rescue of British (and then French) soldiers in 1940. It should be noted that the film, like the Brexiteers, omits the indispensable role played by the French soldiers in enabling the evacuation to take place. The newspapers that supported Brexit, and the tweets of the Brexiteers since the film was released, developed the theme of this 'Dunkirk spirit'. This supposedly was to allow the British to enter into negotiations from a position of strength and make a success of Brexit against anyone and everyone. This approach echoes the assertion made from the beginning that 'they need us more than we need them'– a slogan that has been shown to be unrealistic when dealing with the biggest trading block in the world (one which remained unified throughout).

The second film that resonated with Brexiteers was *Darkest Hour*, also from 2017, directed by Joe Wright. The focus of the film is the spirit of resistance and heroism of one man in the most difficult of times, who changed the destiny of the UK and Europe – Winston Churchill. Viewed by many as the greatest of all British heroes and an emblematic figure of modern times, whose words are still quoted today in order to embellish the speeches of British citizens, Churchill is posthumously enjoying a huge surge in popularity. In his biography of Winston Church-ill, entitled *The Churchill Factor*[5], Boris Johnson creates a strik-ing portrait of his subject, one which bears a strong resemblance to... himself.

The corollary of the Britain that saved Europe is the hatred of Germany and contempt for the so-called cowardice – not to mention collaboration – of those who allowed themselves to be occupied. Here, the main target is France (upon which I shall elaborate in a later chapter). As we know, the Saxe-Cobourg and Gotha dynasty, which changed its name to the very Eng-lish 'Windsor' during the growing anti-German sentiment at the time of the First World War has, in fact, little English blood. When the Queen, then Princess Elizabeth, made it known that she wished to marry Philip of Battenberg, a Prince of Greece and of Denmark from the Danish–German House of Schleswig-Hol-stein-Sonderburg-Glücksburg, there was quite a reaction. Note was made, at the end of the war, of the Nazi sympathies of his sisters and brothers-in-law, who had remained in Germany. Then there were the well-known opinions of the ephemeral and nefar-ious King Edward VIII, who visited Germany with Wallis Simp-son in 1937; the young couple went to Berchtesgaden where a photo shows them standing next to the Führer. The Duke of Windsor, the name he took after his abdication, even included a visit to an SS training camp on this trip.

The continuing British hatred of the Germans was illustrated by a story told by a former German ambassador in London who, one day, exasperated at constantly reading references to Nazis instead of Germans in a certain tabloid newspaper, decided to pay a visit to the editor-in-chief to make a complaint. The meeting was friendly and fruitful – so thought the Ambassador – thereby making his visit worthwhile. He told me that the next day he found an article on his desk from the same newspaper with the alleged heading: 'The Hun came to defend the Nazis and left clicking his heels'. Another example of such anti-German attitudes that remain apparent in Britain comes in the form of Bill Cash, an MP and long-time Europhobe, who was one of the most virulent Brexiteers. His father was killed towards the end of the war and he does not hide his abhorrence of the Germans or his refusal to accept a Europe under the German boot.

The theme of a Fourth Reich, presented as Hitler's revenge for the military failure of the Second World War using the peaceful means of the European Union, is a popular topic in pubs. This makes it easier to understand why my German counterpart in London was extremely cautious – not to say silent – when it came to promoting or defending the European project during the referendum campaign. It is, incidentally, strange that the country that was not occupied feels this hatred towards Germany more strongly than the countries that actually suffered under Nazi occupation; a *mea culpa* from Berlin made it possible for Paris, Brussels or the Hague to take a different view of today's Germany. For many British people, the period of the war remains pivotal and is constantly being examined in the rearview mirror.

The United Kingdom seems to be fond of commemorations and of examining its past and itself. I was struck, when browsing in London's bookshops, by the navel-gazing habits of the British, and especially the English. In addition to numerous books on the two world wars and the nation's history, common in most countries, the tables were often covered with books on identity. Who are we? A form of introspection reflecting an identity crisis. This applies more particularly to the English, a majority of whom voted for Brexit at a time of growing English nation-alism, in the name of which, the young Member of Parliament Jo Cox was murdered. In French bookshops, there are books on the history of France but not, or not many, on the French. If there are such, they are by British academics, like the *Histoire des Passions Françaises* written in several volumes by the Oxford historian Theodore Zeldin.[6] It is the topic of 'Englishness' rather than 'Britishness' that seems to be the most common. Polls have shown that people who call themselves British are more likely to admit to possessing several identities at once – English, Welsh, Irish, Scottish, European – whereas those who think of them-selves as simply English, cannot conceive of being European. Many English Brexiteers are only interested in the destiny of England, considering that Ireland has always been a source of problems for them, therefore any break-up would be welcome. (Their feelings towards Scotland are similar.)

The Scottish independence referendum of 2014 also reacti-vated the 'English question'. Back in 1999, Tony Blair pursued a policy of devolution, setting up parliaments in the three other nations of the United Kingdom – Holyrood in Edinburgh, Stor-mont in Belfast and the Senedd in Cardiff. These assemblies, given wider legislative powers, have become more and more active. If the representatives of the three nations remain, never-theless, frustrated that the Westminster Parliament adopts legis-lation concerning them, the English feel equally frustrated not to have their own Parliament and that Welsh, Irish or Scottish MPs (the last-mentioned favoured by the electoral system), are called upon to pronounce on subjects which concern the English alone.

In September 1946, when giving a speech in Zürich at the dawn of the Cold War, Churchill advocated the constitution of a United States of Europe, saying that 'If Europe were once united in the sharing of its common inheritance there would be no limit to the happiness, prosperity and glory which its 300 or 400 million people would enjoy.' However, his plan was not for the United Kingdom to form part of this Europe but rather support it, like a benevolent power. The former British prime minister saw his country as being at the crossroads of three worlds: the Atlantic, the Commonwealth, and Europe, with priority given firmly to the first of these. This was before the failure of the Suez expedition which resulted in a loss of influence for London and Paris and the emergence of a new world balance. The conclusions drawn from this failure differed over time for the two protagonists: while Paris concluded that it was essential to strengthen its independence, London felt, on the contrary, that it had to place itself under the protection of the United States.

* * *

The argument that the EU has brought peace has, we were often told in London, never worked in the UK, and is indeed beginning to lose some of its force in other member states. Worse, in these times of exacerbated nationalism, its mere mention gives rise to extremely violent reactions. Against all the evidence, there is a refusal to concede that the EU has made it possible for the members of the European Union to live in peace for over 70 years on the basis of a Franco–German reconciliation. The explicit aim of the European Coal and Steel Community (ECSC) – the precursor of the EU – as solemnly stated by Robert Schuman in the *Salon de l'Horloge* of the *Quai d'Orsay* on 9 May 1950 was to make war between the European powers 'not merely unthinkable, but materially impossible'. Guy Verhofstadt referenced the link between the European Union and peace on the centenary of the First World War, echoing Winston Churchill's 'jaw jaw better than war war' by posting 'Once we fought, now we talk' on Facebook. Interestingly, David Cameron, according to his Director of Communications Craig Oliver, explicitly forbade any reference to this link at the commemoration of the end of the First World War.

Contrary to popular belief, the theme of peace was indeed present in the early days of the UK's membership. As pointed out by Fintan O'Toole,[7] those voting in the referendum of 1975, which resulted in a large majority in favour of the European Union, had known the war and learned the lesson that nationalism was dangerous – the United Kingdom could not ignore what was happening on the continent. In 1975, the pro-European campaign 'Britain in Europe' included a reference to the poppy, the red flower of remembrance, and used the logo of the dove of peace; slogans included 'On VE Day we celebrated the beginnings of peace. Vote yes to make sure we keep it'. Veterans to whom I awarded the *Légion d'Honneur* still say today that they were fighting for Europe. It is strange that references of this type are still being made by Boris Johnson.

The fact that the last conflict in Western Europe was between loyalists and nationalists in Northern Ireland does not even seem to occur to those who despise the European Union. Notwithstanding, this conflict, which lasted 30 years and resulted in 3,500 victims, was violent and murderous on the territory of Northern Ireland and in England. It struck at the heart of British power, right up to the royal family – Lord Mountbatten, great-grandson of Queen Victoria, last Viceroy of India, uncle and godfather to Prince Charles, was killed by the IRA in August 1979, while the Queen herself escaped an attempt in Australia in 1970. In 1984, a bomb intended for Margaret Thatcher killed five people in a large Brighton hotel where the Conservative Party Conference was being held. It does not seem to occur either to partisans of Brexit that tensions began to ease, as pointed out by Kevin O'Rourke,[8] even before the Good Friday Agreement of 10 April 1998, when emissaries from both north and south of the Irish border met in Brussels, laying the basis for the peace process.

Arguably, it was membership of the European Union that allowed friendly relations to develop (the dismantling of physical borders also helped). Although it was not the EU that concluded the Good Friday Agreement, President Clinton's special envoy, George Mitchell, said that negotiations would never have taken place without the EU. Furthermore, Brussels remains the guarantor and the generous financier of this peace agreement. In spite of this, the subject was carefully avoided during the referendum campaign.

As for relations between London and the Europeans, the history of the country as told by Brexiteers is that of a poor little United Kingdom, oppressed by the EU. The European project, in any case, was doomed. For the Conservatives, it was a socialist undertaking; for Labour, a capitalist plot. Both political parties, over the course of their respective mandates, have changed their position on whether or not to support the European Union. It was unlucky that Jeremy Corbyn was elected leader of the Labour Party at the same time as Eurosceptics were in the ascendant in the Conservative Party. While Corbyn did not openly declare himself to be anti-European Union, he managed to maintain such ambiguity on the subject that his supporters did not really know what the Labour Party's position was, although perhaps they understood intuitively that their leader was in favour of Brexit.

The heroine of the Eurosceptics in the Tory Party is Margaret Thatcher with her famous demand of 'I want my money back', and the speech she gave in Bruges in September 1988 in which she fiercely opposed the federalist proposals of Jacques Delors. They forget that she was an ardent Europhile in the first years of membership and argued the case for a common market that her successors were keen to implement fully. In 1975, Thatcher even said she supported the European Union from the bottom of her heart, adding that it was the constant European vision of the Conservative Party. She went on to quote Disraeli, stating 'if that country, from a perverse interpretation of its insular geographical position, turns an indifferent ear to the feelings and the fortunes of continental Europe, such a course would, I believe, only end in its becoming an object of general plunder'.[9] Even the famous Bruges speech, presented by Brexiteers as the Thatcherite position on Europe, was more a rejection of a federal vision rather than of the European Union itself. It is true that once out of power, Margaret Thatcher never ceased to complicate the life of her successor, John Major, especially with regard to this subject, rallying to the Eurosceptic camp.

To say that the United Kingdom had no influence within the European Union in 2016 is the opposite of the truth. Europe has benefited from the input of top British experts on all domains (trade, agriculture, fisheries, finance, military and so on) who left their mark by pushing the EU further towards liberalism. You only need to ask the French, ever ready to criticise the EU's shift towards Anglo-Saxon liberalism, more so in that the British succeeded in being given responsibilities within the institutions for matters of trade.

A few important names come to mind when considering the UK's influence within the EU: Roy Jenkins, who was president of the Commission from 1977 to 1981; Leon Brittan, several times a commissioner for competition, trade, then external affairs, before becoming vice-president between 1989 and 1999; Chris Patten, former Conservative Party chairman who led them to victory, the famous last governor of Hong Kong, commissioner for external affairs from 1999 to 2004, and today chancellor of the University of Oxford; Peter Mandelson, the famous and influential 'Prince of Darkness', of redoubtable intelligence, commissioner for trade between 2004 and 2008; Paddy Ashdown, former leader of the Liberal Democrats who was high representative for Bosnia and Herzegovina, on behalf of both the European Union and the United Nations; and lastly Jonathan Hill, former leader of the House of Lords, commissioner for financial stability, financial services and Capital Markets Union between 2014 and 2016, who resigned following the referendum victory of the Brexiteers. Europol, the European agency for police co-operation, was headed with *brio* by the British national Rob

Wainwright for nine years, and the Joint Situation Centre – the embryo of a European information service – was set up by William Shapcott. Two British vice admirals effectively directed one of the most successful operations of the European Union from the military base of Northwood: the eradication of piracy in the Indian Ocean by the Atalanta naval force. When I visited them at their headquarters, they were all very proud of this achievement. But because of Brexit, operations had to be transferred to Spain and France. The expertise of the British officers on the military committee in Brussels was particularly appreciated.

Excellent permanent representatives of Her Majesty, influential and respected by their peers, the best officials of the Foreign Office, served in Brussels. Amongst those I was acquainted with were David Hannay, now in the House of Lords who was, when I knew him, one of the rising stars of the Security Council in New York; John Kerr, also in the House of Lords, who revealed that he was involved in the drafting of Article 50, regulating how a country leaves the EU, never thinking that it would be used one day for his own country; Kim Darroch, who unintentionally shot to fame as ambassador to Washington after being thrown under the bus by Boris Johnson, who failed to defend him after one of his diplomatic communications was leaked – where he described the Trump administration as dysfunctional and inept – which unsurprisingly made Trump furious; and Yvan Rogers, the bearer of bad news who made the mistake of explaining to Theresa May, based on his expertise in European matters, that the Brexit process would be long and complex. Their unfailing expertise, rigour, creativity and sharp wit (not to mention their mastery of the English language – it is not easy to use the language of Shakespeare correctly in the context of the technocratic jargon of Brussels) meant that their colleagues turned to them when looking for compromise solutions. Contrary to the claims of the Brexiteers, Britain's public servants acted in accordance with their instructions and delivered their opinions on the proposals of the Commission. Indeed, it is the role of the Commission to make proposals, and the role of member states to make decisions; it is not faceless Brussels bureaucrats who make decisions that are contrary to British interests.

Needless to say, the anecdotes of Boris Johnson, who was a correspondent for *The Daily Telegraph* in Brussels between 1989 and 1994, that detailed the EU ban on shrimp crisps or the recycling of tea bags, were nothing more than little made-up stories designed to ridicule the Brussels bureaucracy while entertaining his readers. This was after he was dismissed by *The Times* for telling blatant lies. nicknamed 'the buffoon', his 'Euromyths' – 'fake news' before the term existed – which varyingly elicited annoyance, amusement or shrugging of shoulders from his colleagues, did more harm than serious journalists realised at the time. They, unfortunately, helped create an image of a monstrous European bureaucracy, drowning in red tape, absurd and prescriptive.

Therefore, no one was surprised or upset when, as a candidate for the post of prime minister in 2019, feigning indignation, he brandished a kipper that he claimed the European Union ordered the fishermen of the Isle of Man to keep wrapped in ice (even though the Isle of Man was not a member of the European Union and, better yet, this would fall under national, not community, jurisdiction). Ironically, it is the British who are known for over-regulating when implementing European directives.

In any event, it has been a while since the Western world entered into the 'post-truth' era – an expression that was 'word of the year' in 2016 in the prestigious Oxford dictionary – or one of 'alternative facts'. This term was used by Donald Trump's spokesperson Kellyane Conway in relation to the record attendance claimed for the President's inauguration ceremony, in complete contradiction to the pictures shown. She was no doubt unaware that she was quoting the British author George Orwell – unsurprisingly, sales of his frighteningly excellent dystopian novel *1984* have significantly increased of late.

A well-known myth, at least on this side of the Atlantic, is that of a special relationship with the United States based on Winston Churchill's oft-repeated assertion made to General de Gaulle in 1944: 'each time we must choose between Europe and the open sea...we shall always be for the open sea'.[10] The choice was, in fact, between Eisenhower and de Gaulle. Conceptualised in 1946 by Winston Churchill in his Missouri speech (famous for its reference to the Iron Curtain) the so-called special relationship has evolved over the years through a series of military agreements – notably nuclear ones – and agreements on the sharing of intelligence (the 'Five Eyes Alliance', including also Canada, Australia and New Zealand). A need for reassurance on the United Kingdom's part after the failure of the Suez expedition or at the time of the Iraq war? Supported by close relations between leaders on each side of the Atlantic – Margaret Thatcher and Ronald Reagan, Tony Blair and George Bush – it has also given rise to suspicion and criticism. By deciding to side with the American President, whatever the cost, in the catastrophic war with Iraq, Tony Blair, a prime minister who marked the history of his country while also enjoying particular admiration in Europe, was caricatured as Bush's poodle. His reputation was left in tatters; his sensible arguments against Brexit and calls for a second referendum ignored.

Above all, this relationship between the US and UK is profoundly asymmetric. While the United Kingdom needs the United States for its defence, as far as Washington is concerned, the UK is only a junior or subsidiary partner with whom communication is made easy since both speak English (even though, as George Bernard Shaw so rightly said 'England and America are two countries separated by a common language'). The Americans are amused by this constant reference to a special relationship, although they sometimes also use it out of politeness. Obama's former adviser Jeremy Shapiro admitted that for the United States, the concept had little importance – American leaders take care to refer to it at press conferences when the

British are present, but otherwise view it as a bit of a joke. Donald Trump took the same cynical view of the relationship even if, from time to time, he alluded to it as much to annoy the Europeans and Remainers, whom he detested, as to please his populist counterpart Boris Johnson. Trump promised him a fast-tracked free trade agreement, the terms of which would certainly not have been favourable to the British given the power balance between the two.

When I was serving in the French Mission to the United Nations in the 1990s, I was struck by an off-the-cuff remark made by one of my colleagues, as English as they come, who said that it was since coming to live in the United States that he felt himself to be European. Yet this was in New York in the Clinton era, and not Trump's *Amérique profonde* (American heartland). Since then, the gap has widened further – the 45th President of the United States was held in contempt by the elite and youth of Britain due to his blatant use of racism, misogyny and vulgarity.

The contrast between the official visit of the President to Paris for the 14 July celebrations in 2017, which elicited no public criticism, and his planned or actual visits to London, which provoked demonstrations of unprecedented hostility, is rather striking. When, soon after taking up office, Theresa May hurried to Washington and then invited the President for a state visit, the centre of London was in turmoil, blocked by mass protests. The main argument was that such a visit would be an insult to the Queen. For his part, the Speaker of the House of Commons said he would not receive anyone so racist and misogynistic in the Parliament of Westminster. The mayor of London, who had not appreciated Trump's opinions regarding Muslims or the personal insults made against him, also objected. Given the risks involved, the state visit was postponed. An official visit took place later in 2018 and had to be confined to Windsor, while the infamous balloon depicting Trump as a pink, podgy baby with a huge slick of yellow hair, wearing a nappy floated above London. The state visit finally took place in 2019, and baby Trump was back in the sky.

The embarrassment and opposition are indeed linked to the fact that the two countries are separated by a common language as previously mentioned, and a filial bond of which the UK is slightly ashamed. *If Only They Didn't Speak English*[11] is the title of a book by Jon Sopel, BBC correspondent in Washington for several years. Particularly in relation to the election of Donald Trump, the argument of the book was that more normal relations would thereby be facilitated. Jon Sopel calls this 'unrequited love' on the part of the British since apart from royal events, which fascinate the Americans, the latter are more or less indifferent to political life in Britain. The election of David Cameron in 2010 was, according to Sopel, not even mentioned in the television news broadcasts in America.

It is true that Trump found favour with Nigel Farage and Boris Johnson. Farage because of an affinity that led the American President to urge the Government to appoint him ambassador to Washington, and later to suggest a Farage–Johnson alliance for the general election of December 2019 (something which did not, incidentally, elicit protestations of interference from the Brexiteers). For Johnson, it was more a case of needing to have something to show for his 'fantastic Brexit'. Having said that, even if his classical education sets him apart, Boris Johnson is surely fascinated by the man who so closely resembles him, both in his populist style and buffoonery as by his tousled yellow hair.

The Prime Minister needs to prove that a favourable free trade agreement with Washington is possible. In reality, however, this puts Britain in a state of greater dependence than with the EU, where it had a place at the negotiating table on a par with everyone else. As is said in diplomatic circles: if you are not at the table, that means you are on the menu. As usual, Trump blew hot and cold, announcing a formidable free trade agreement, then saying that the health service, to which the British are so attached, could be partially privatised, and lastly warning that the British could say goodbye to any agreement if they persisted in taxing GAFAM (Google, Apple, Facebook, Amazon, Microsoft). The threat became clearer still in the context of the trade war with China over using Huawei for the system of communications in Britain; London had to backtrack, withdrawing the authorisation already granted to Huawei on certain conditions. As for compliance with health standards and the protection of British consumers, it is clear that this was not a priority for Trump – chlorinated chicken would have been on British menus. All this for the sake of Brexit! Even if members of the British Cabinet periodically felt obliged to say they would not accept such conditions, this blackmail didn't seem to bother the Brexiteers, who had been so indignant at Obama's intervention when he warned that in the event of Brexit, Britain risked going to 'the back of the queue' regarding negotiation of a free trade agreement. Is this really what taking back control meant?

Whether it likes it or not, the future of the United Kingdom will be determined much more by Europe than by the rest of the world. Even David Cameron in his Bloomberg speech in January 2013, which announced the referendum, made reference to the fact with this ringing declaration: 'From Caesar's legions to the Napoleonic Wars. From the Reformation, the Enlightenment and the Industrial Revolution to the defeat of Nazism. We have helped to write European history, and Europe has helped write ours.' So actually, with Brexit, London has broken with its history and its constant policy of ensuring that no continental alliance is formed against it. The European concert, as conceptualised by the Scottish philosopher David Hume in the 18th century, was characterised by the balancing of powers so as to ensure the security of the United Kingdom. Now, the UK has caused a continental block of 27 countries to join forces against it – Napoleon's infamous blockade, which England was so afraid of. No doubt the UK's leaders thought they could again 'divide and rule' as Sir Humphrey, in the remarkable BBC cult television series *Yes Minister* – indispensable for an understanding of English political life – cynically explained to the newly appointed minister. Sir Humphrey stated that the reason the UK joined the European Union in 1973 was so that it could, from the inside, pit the French against the Germans, the Germans against the Italians, and so on. In reality, before the start of Brexit negotiations, Michael Barnier's deputy explained to the French ambassadors in Europe that while every European country could, in relation to a particular subject, have an interest in reaching an advantageous bilateral agreement with London, this was not the case for the spectrum of the relationship as a whole. While London claimed to hold all the cards, the solidarity of the 27 held firm, not through ideology, dogmatism or a desire to punish, but simply through pragmatism and well-understood self-interest.

Dreaming of the return to a glorious past, the United Kingdom also, paradoxically, presents itself as a victim of the European Union. Some even feel that their country has been made a vassal of the Commission, their *bête noire*, as had happened long ago with the catholic monarchs. Henry VIII took back control by breaking with Rome, confiscating all the Church's assets while he was at it. A breaking away from the continent – a first Brexit? The primary reason was personal: to divorce Catherine of Aragon in order to marry Ann Boleyn.

A cartoon strip that did the rounds of social media provided a perfect example of this attitude of arrogance combined with a victim mentality. In the first picture, a man with a wide, mocking smile says, 'You need us more than we need you'; in the second, the smile is not so wide but he still says, 'The United Kingdom will have its cake and eat it too'; in the third, the man has a put-upon expression, complaining, 'You bully us'. This is what the British themselves call a 'reality check', even though Boris Johnson may be tempted by a return to hubris and 'magical thinking'.

It is also this conviction of exceptionalism and the desire to pursue policies different from those of other European countries that formed the basis of Boris Johnson's management of the health crisis in the spring of 2020. The least that can be said is that the results have been less than convincing and have given rise to sharp criticism, even amongst his own supporters.

CHAPTER 3

'That Sweet Enemy'

THE OXYMORONIC TITLE of a book by the Cambridge historian, Robert Tombs and his French wife Isabelle, *That Sweet Enemy* – also sung by the poet Philip Sidney in the 16th century – perfectly illustrates the unique relationship between the United Kingdom and France.[i] The two are closely intertwined (until 1801, the kings of England also bore the title king of France) and were periodically at war over centuries. Although they have been at peace for over 200 years, their attraction-rejection rivalry has never ceased – sometimes with humour, sometimes not.

In 2003 in the United Nations Security Council, French Foreign Minister Dominique de Villepin made a famous speech arguing against intervention in Iraq, but he began by saying 'It is an old country, France, in an old continent, Europe...'. In response, his British counterpart, Jack Straw, pursuing a policy radically opposed to France's, began his own speech with humour echoing the ringing tones of de Villepin's: 'I come from an old country founded by France.' Straw later admitted he had wondered about saying 'invaded by France'.

England's real date of birth is 14 October 1066 when William the Conqueror, from Falaise in Normandy, beat the Saxon King Harold at the Battle of Hastings. A somewhat ambiguous birth certificate, since it was a French (Norman) victory, the epic story is depicted in the Bayeux Tapestry.[i] It is this fact that led

---

[i] President Macron pledged that this masterpiece of Romanesque art, often considered to be the forerunner of cartoon strips, will be given on loan to the United Kingdom.

Georges Clemenceau to say that England was 'a French colony which turned out badly'.[2]

In October 2016, I was invited to the small town of Battle, to the very place where King Harold was killed, for a commemoration of the 950th anniversary of the event. This was organised by the 1066 Association, run by charming gentlemen of a certain age, who had arranged for a pleasant reception followed by a costumed re-enactment of the battle the next day. The Home Secretary and Member of Parliament for Hastings Amber Rudd was present; afterwards, we were all invited to add an embroidery stitch to the long linen cloth reconstituting the final missing scenes of the original tapestry, which represented the history of the town after the battle. A pretty wooden jigsaw of this embroidery was presented to me, which I finished doing over a rainy weekend in London. It was a friendly, good-natured but relatively discreet event – almost covert – so I was astonished to see a photo of the costumed re-enactment on the front page of the *Financial Times* the next day.[3] But it was nothing compared to the publicity and the resources deployed for the official commemorations of the symbolic victories against the French: Agincourt, Trafalgar, and especially Waterloo.

The Norman influence in England was strong and long-lasting as regards political and social organisation, but also the language since the Norman nobility spoke French for 200 years. Georges Clemenceau also made a sarcastic comment with this in mind, describing English as 'badly spoken French'. English only became a written language because of the Hundred Years War in the Late Middle Ages, as it was deemed intolerable to use the language of the enemy. Jealously fighting today against the use of English – which, despite our best efforts, has become the world's *lingua franca* – and anglicisms, we French forget that 40 per cent of modern English words (ie thousands of them) are of French origin. This is especially prevalent in the fields of law and politics, including the word 'Parliament', which incarnates the supreme and indisputable political authority, as Brexiteers proclaimed end-lessly during the campaign. The Westminster Parliament, together with Big Ben, has become the emblem of London and is proudly protected by Richard the Lionheart, son of Eleanor of Aquitaine, on his horse of stone. Upon arriving in London, I wondered about the origin of the name 'Portcullis' given to a modern extension of the Parliament building where MPS receive visitors – including ambassadors – to their offices, or in the landscaped atrium where they can hear the bell requiring their presence in the House for a vote. This rather unusual name, in fact, comes from the French *porte coulissante* (sliding door). The motto on the Queen's coat of arms *Dieu et mon droit* (God and my right) is French, as is *Honni soit qui mal y pense* (Shame on him who thinks ill of it). The approval given by the Queen to acts of Parliament is in French also – *La reyne le veult* (the Queen wills it).

The English language includes many Saxon words and their Norman equivalent. An interesting little fact is that the words for living animals – sheep, cow, calf – are of Saxon origin; whereas those for the same animals prepared for eating, which only the aristocracy could afford, are Norman in origin – mutton, beef and veal (*mouton, boeuf, veau*). Incidentally, the menus for state dinners served in Buckingham Palace are written in French and the food is served on turquoise Sèvres porcelain (offered to the Duchess of Manchester by Louis XVI). Talleyrand, who was the ambassador in London between 1830 and 1834 and whose majestic portrait hung in the stairway of the French Residence in my time, still communicated with the British Foreign Office in French. It was only in 1834 that Foreign Minister Lord Palmerston, a distinguished and enthusiastic advocate of British power, decided to impose English as the language to be used in diplomatic correspondence. The black and white cat in the Foreign Office, Diplocat, who has been given a Twitter account and is responsible for dealing with the many mice in the august old building, has been named after Palmerston. During the referendum campaign, the little mouser was very seriously accused by one MP of being a secret agent for Brussels and having a spy chip inserted! He is thus on an equal footing with his illustrious neighbour, Larry, the 10 Downing Street cat who, on his own Twitter account, often takes a dissident stance, adopting positions different from those of the owner of the premises.

We often may not realise that words that sound typically English in fact derive from French – the word 'foreign(er)', so often heard during the referendum campaign, comes from the French word *forain* (meaning 'itinerant'). In addition to words or expressions with such historic roots, there are others which have been adopted more recently because they sound chic – raison d'être, rendez-vous, déjà-vu, and so on. A dominant language that is becoming less obsessed about protecting against foreign input. Just before leaving China to take up my post in London, when I expressed the worry that I might not be able to remember a particular word when being interviewed in English, my British counterpart in Beijing advised me, in that case, to resort to French – supposedly, interviewers or listeners would be flattered to be considered as cultured people who understood the language. This was, incidentally, the advice given to Alice by the Red Queen: 'Speak in French when you can't remember the English for a thing'.[4]

The royal family preserves a special link with the French culture and language. The Queen Mother's love of France and all things French has been transmitted to her daughter – Queen Elizabeth takes pleasure in speaking French, which she does very well indeed. She also appreciates the country, to which she has been invited five times on state visits (in addition to this she has been on several private visits in order to purchase horses). This love seems to be mutual as she has been welcomed enthusiastically by the French – the flower market by the river Seine has even been named after her. Prince Charles, whom I had invited to visit the French warship in Cardiff Bay during the NATO summit of September 2014 in Newport, let it be known that he wished to speak to the sailors in French. In May 2015, Princess Anne attended the ceremony celebrating the centenary of the French *Lycée* in London – rechristened the *Lycée Charles-de-Gaulle* in 1980 – speaking to the pupils in my native language, in memory of her French teacher who had attended this prestigious school. This tradition is unfortunately no longer being followed by the younger generation of royals. I had thought to propose the services of a French governess for little Prince George, third in line to the throne, and Princess Charlotte, born during my time in London, but it proved too complicated in these times to arrange – a pity.

France is surrounded by many neighbours, natural targets for our prejudices and jokes which are distributed more or less equally amongst them. As far as our 'hereditary enemy' is concerned, the accusation of duplicity and hypocrisy is reflected in the expression *'perfide Albion'* (perfidious England/Great Britain) which dates back to Bossuet and Mme de Sévigné in the 17th century. It became widespread in the 19th century with a popular cartoon series, *La Famille Fenouillard*, in which everything was the fault of *'La Perfide Albion qui a brûlé Jeanne d'Arc sur le rocher de Sainte-Hélène'* (Perfidious Albion which burnt Joan of Arc on the rock of Saint Helena).[5] But, since France is really the only large neighbour Britain has, this feeds into an apparent obsession with the French and consequential 'French bashing'. The saying 'Always blame the French' has in fact been in use since the Middle Ages, and this attitude has become part of British culture, sometimes accompanied with humour but not always. And not only British culture, but other English-speaking cultures too, since the same disparagement exists on the other side of the Atlantic and, after the sensitive period of our disagreements over the 2003 war against Iraq, now focuses on our supposed aversion to globalisation, liberalism, and even entrepreneurship. In an episode of *Yes Minister*, the very 'Oxford' Permanent Secretary Sir Humphrey, asks the Prime Minister about his visit to Washington. The latter replies, with a satisfied and amused air, that everything went very well – he and the American President began by each reading out his notes, then swapped them so as not to waste time in starting the 'usual French bashing'.

Calais, by a twist of historical fate, is the most important crossing point between our two countries. On her deathbed, Mary Tudor – Bloody Mary – said that if her heart were cut open, the name Calais would be found engraved upon it since, after 211 years of English occupation, the town had been reconquered by the Duke of Guise and reverted to the French crown in 1558. In fact, Calais continues to be a thorn in the side because of its 'Jungle' (unauthorised migrant encampments) and the violent and often fatal attempts made by migrants to reach London. When I arrived in the United Kingdom, little mention was yet being made of the problem in France, at least at national level, whereas every day British television showed pictures of gangs of young migrants mounting attacks on lorries with UK registration plates. I had to explain the situation on television on several occasions to journalists who accused France of, firstly, being incapable of preventing these attempts; then – after increased levels of security had been agreed between Theresa May and Bernard Cazeneuve in August 2015 – of allowing migrants to live in inhumane conditions in unspeakable hovels; and lastly – when we cleared the southern zone and rehoused the migrants in permanent accommodation with improved living conditions – of destroying what said journalists all of a sudden seemed to view as a marvellous and convivial place to live. Understand that, if you can.

Every Friday night during this period, dozens of 'No Borders' anarchists took the train from St Pancras to Calais in order to convince the migrants to make every effort to cross to the United Kingdom, where they were told they were expected and would be well received. This was a mission shared – some of them in good faith – with gangs of people smugglers, whose interests lay elsewhere than the welfare of the migrants. The activists returned to London on Sunday night, mission accomplished, and the migrants continued to risk their lives in an attempt to reach what they were led to believe was a place of refuge.

This became a red-hot topic during the referendum campaign in which hostility to immigration was a key factor. David Cameron tried, unsuccessfully, to convince voters that if the UK left the European Union, France would renege on the bilateral *Le Touquet* agreement of 2003 – which made the French police responsible for security – and would push the border across the Channel to Dover, which would see massive arrivals of migrants. The situation seemed to calm down when France destroyed the Jungle once and for all, relocated most of the migrants to other regions of the country and cooperated with the United Kingdom in processing persons with families, and unaccompanied minors. This was in accordance with the Dubs Amendment, named after Lord Dubs who, at the age of six, was put on one of the *Kindertransport* – trains of Jewish children fleeing the Nazis – destined for Great Britain. Of course, this is not the end of the story since even though the Jungle has been razed to the ground and the migrants relocated elsewhere throughout France, the British have agreed to take in some of them. Those that continue to arrive on French soil are mostly from Sudan, Somalia, Eritrea or Afghanistan; they speak English and wish to emigrate to the United Kingdom where there are already large communities from their home countries. Attempts to cross the Channel since then have been made on small boats. This exasperated Brexiteers, once again encouraged by Nigel Farage who railed against an invasion; whereas, there continues to be a well-established system of cooperation between the British and French authorities. Besides which, the number of potential migrants still seeking refuge in the UK is well below the requests for asylum in France, or Germany.

Let us not forget that, well before this, English people opposed to any opening of borders towards the continent objected to the construction of the tunnel under the Channel, on the pretext that England would be swamped by rabies-infected French foxes.

Calais is not the only name that evokes strong feelings amongst the English. There are all those battles in relation to which the French writer Alphonse Allais said that the English were really very strange since, unlike us, they name their streets and squares after defeats – Trafalgar, Waterloo.... It seems as though every club, refectory or student halls of residence bears the name of one of these glorious victories over France. Even the most Francophile of peers in the House of Lords cannot resist the pleasure, when we are invited for lunch or afternoon tea, of showing off the painting of the Battle of Trafalgar which hangs in pride of place in the cosy dining hall.

Emotions reached fever-pitch in England in 2015 in the run-up to the commemoration of the 200th anniversary of the Battle of Waterloo, which was a strange experience for me. People were so passionate that I had the impression that the battle (which I had no strong feelings towards myself) took place not 200, but two years previously. Napoleon was often compared to Hitler, or at least perceived essentially as a blood-thirsty conqueror, as if Great Britain's allies against him – the Austro-Hungarian Empire, Prussia and Russia – were at the time progressive democracies. The tabloid newspapers were particularly virulent, accusing me of supporting his attempted conquest of Europe or, better still, of denying that Napoleon was defeated at Waterloo. Stephen Clarke, who had previously published *1000 years of Annoying the French*,[6] brought out a new book for the occasion with the humorous title, *How the French Won Waterloo (or Think They Did)*.[7]

The fact remains that the six months preceding the commemoration provided the opportunity for constant criticisms and remarks, not all of them in the best of taste. References were made to the battle in the opening jokes of speeches, even those made by the clergy, for example the sermon given at Oxford – in Latin – at the prestigious ceremony of the awarding of doctorates *honoris causa*, to which I had been invited by Chancellor Chris Patten. In the British Museum, an exhibition of particularly brutal cartoons by George Cruikshank and Thomas Rowlandson, depicting the Corsican spider in his web, illustrated the degree of ill-feeling felt by the English towards the man they called Bonaparte, or 'Little

Boney', to try to belittle or ridicule their charismatic enemy. The exhibition was inaugurated by the highly respected Director of the British Museum Neil Macgregor, and the wonderful author Julian Barnes (who is both Francophone and a Francophile). The latter, justifiably considered to be the 'permanent French ambassador to the United Kingdom', who always describes the French with both tenderness and humour, and to whom I had the privilege of awarding the *Légion d'Honneur* at the French Residence. He gave a humorous and subtle speech in which he highlighted Napoleon's exceptional qualities as an administrator.

I had accepted the kind, personal invitation to the commemoration ceremonies extended to me by the Wellesley's – descendants of the Duke of Wellington – to celebrate, in a spirit of friendship, 200 years of peace between our countries. As it happens, this coincided with a symbolic date for us, if ever there was one, and earlier that morning I presided over the annual ceremony to commemorate the call to arms of 18 June 1940 by General de Gaulle. This took place at the foot of his statue, unveiled in 1993 by the Queen Mother in Carlton Gardens, where his headquarters were located during the war, and where you can still visit his refurbished office adorned with a Free French flag. Afterwards I attended the memorial service in Westminster Abbey, where the royal family were also present.

In the evening, I attended a banquet for some 700 guests at Guildhall where, to general applause, a descendant of the Prussian Marshal Blücher, just as his ancestor arrived in the middle of the battle, arrived minutes before the main dish was served, which was beef Wellington, of course. This was followed by a dessert called, in the interests of parity, 'millefeuille Napoleon'. When leaving, a German colleague joked that it was nice – for once – to be on the right side, which made me think that every year, our German counterparts see it as their duty to attend our victory ceremonies at the Cenotaph in London, or before other monuments to the dead throughout the world. I was not at the annual banquet that replicates the one served to celebrate the victory of 18 June 1815 at Apsley House, the home of the Dukes of Wellington. But I have had the opportunity to visit this unique place, at the entrance to Hyde Park, where the address is simply 'Number One, London', and where there is an obvious obsession with the great Corsican. Portraits of Napoleon and his wife Josephine adorn the walls, and there is a gigantic statue by Canova of Napoleon portrayed as Mars – naked and unarmed, the peacemaker – waiting by the stairway to welcome visitors.

Other locations, other narratives or storytelling clearly show that history is made up as much of interpretations as it is of true events. In 2012, the Russians celebrated the bicentenary of the Battle of Borodino (or of Moskova, as the French call it), and the 205th anniversary, on 7 September 2017, coincided with the day of my arrival in Russia. No bitterness there – on the contrary, there is a fascination with the life and times of Napoleon. Families have kept busts of him; re-enactments of the battle are enthusiastically organised at regular intervals. When some months later, in March 2018, I arrived at a palace at the gates of the Russian capital for a lunch to celebrate Mikhail Gorbachev's birthday, the young woman who welcomed me told me with a smile (and something like pride) that it was from one of the rooms of this palace that Napoleon had watched Moscow burn.

Another symbolic battle against the French was, of course, Trafalgar. I was not in London for the bicentenary commemoration in 2005 but in 2015, the day after the *Charlie Hebdo* attack, at the vigil organised by the French community, Trafalgar Square was lit up in the colours of the French flag in honour of the victims. Many British people participated spontaneously, and a little sticker that read '*Je suis Charlie*' had been pasted high up on Nelson's Column itself.

An incredibly moving moment that reflected our shared destiny was the France versus England friendly football match at Wembley, organised immediately following the outrage at the Bataclan and to which I was invited by David Cameron. He was one of the first leaders to agree to participate in the march on

11 January 2015 after the *Charlie Hebdo* attack and the first to place a white rose in remembrance at the scene of the Bataclan tragedy (soon followed by Barack Obama and Angela Merkel). The Prime Minister had also asked for the English and French players to sing the *Marseillaise* together; the words, shown on giant screens, were sung by David Cameron and Prince William as well as Boris Johnson in the stands. In 2017, in the same spirit of solidarity, President Macron in turn invited Theresa May to a friendly match at the *Stade de France* in Saint-Denis after the Westminster and Manchester attacks.

Among the most moving highlights of my mandate was the awarding of the *Légion d'Honneur* to veterans of the Normandy landings. Unlike the American, Canadian and Australian soldiers – many of whom had been awarded this medal – the British had not received this token of gratitude, since there had been no response from the British authorities to a proposal made by President Chirac. It was only on the occasion of the Queen's state visit in June 2014, for the anniversary of the landings, that President Hollande announced, on the beaches of Normandy, all British veterans would be offered the award. Then followed a race against time since, to everyone's surprise, we received nearly 5,000 requests, often relayed through MPS. We had to urgently submit these individual files – each one validated by the British Ministry of Defence – to the *Grande Chancellerie de la Légion d'Honneur* and obtain the corresponding number of medals for these gentlemen, who ranged in age from 90 to 101 years old. Only one woman, who had worked in the decoding services, was a recipient at this time, but other requests were subsequently received which meant that more women with a similar profile were decorated with the honour.

The veterans came to the French Residence with their families – spouses, children and grandchildren – who heard, many for the first time, about their heroic acts as read out by pupils of the 'twin' French *lycées* Charles-de-Gaulle and Winston Churchill. The BBC and other television and radio channels were always present to record their stories and show our appreciation – appreciation that is matched only by the gratitude we owe them. I had difficulty hiding my emotions when these veterans, including some in wheelchairs, stood to attention at the first notes of the *Marseillaise*, some of them singing along. Many returned nearly every year to see the families who had welcomed them in Normandy. Some told me they had hoped not to die before this day of recognition; one man's son confided in me that his father, since deceased, was so proud of receiving the honour that he wore his medal even when he was in the hospital. Many wrote to me to thank France for the honour, and I received touching letters expressing solidarity after the terrorist attacks. Some publicly took a stand against Brexit, which they deemed abhorrent and in total contradiction with their intervention to liberate the continent from Nazi barbarism.

This brotherhood-in-arms was also celebrated during the commemorations of the First World War, particularly at the 100th anniversary of the Battle of the Somme. I arrived in the company of British participants on a special Eurostar which left London early in the morning; it was a simple, dignified and moving ceremony at the cemetery of Thiepval. Charles Dance – the charismatic Shakespearian actor and star of *Game of Thrones,* who also played Lord Mountbatten in *The Crown* – read, in a deep and spellbinding voice, letters written by soldiers to their families, before a cascade of paper poppies and cornflowers were released over the fields of the Somme.

Today, however, the English seem convinced that the French want to punish them for something that they inflicted on themselves, but for which they are unwilling to accept the consequences. Thus, when the time came for the first summer holidays post-Brexit, when there were interminable queues for the ferries due to security measures imposed by both British and French police, British social media was full of complaints about how these measures had been introduced to punish them for Brexit. The word 'punishment' is used often, notably by Boris Johnson who accused France of being at the head of a punishment squad. From time to time grumpy old men, upon hearing French being spoken on the tube, would aggressively accuse the French of cowardice – referring to the period of occupation – and say they were happy to be leaving the European Union, leaving us at the mercy of the Germans. Not all those promoting Brexit are anti-French, far from it, since some of them – such as former Chancellor of the Exchequer Nigel Lawson, or Lord Rothermere, the owner of the *Daily Mail* – were living in our country. Nevertheless, the notion of *forain* was a key component of the Brexit campaign.

The bilateral relations, that are essential for our two countries to function, will have to be rebuilt, particularly because negotiations were conducted exclusively at EU level, deliberately limiting bilateral contacts. Before the COVID-19 pandemic, 12 to 13 million British nationals visited France every year, mostly during the holidays, and the United Kingdom provided France's biggest trade surplus. Strong links have been established with regard to defence and security – 2021 saw the tenth anniversary of the Lancaster House Treaty which, amongst other things, provided for the creation of a combined Franco-British joint expeditionary force of 10,000 soldiers. However, some joint projects, such as the development of combat drones, have already been abandoned and will be pursued with Germany instead. The United Kingdom will no longer be in the same club as France, and will instead look towards other alliances with NATO and the United States. Nothing will be the same as before.

CHAPTER 4

The Campaign: Emotion Versus Reason

WHETHER NATIVE OR foreign, what observer of British political life – usually so orderly and phlegmatic – could have predicted such an outpouring of emotion during the Brexit campaign? There seemed to be general agreement that Europe did not inspire strong feelings in the United Kingdom and that the campaign would be fought simply on the basis of facts versus facts. It was no doubt this that convinced David Cameron, albeit without enthusiasm, that reason would win. Of course, it was expected that the arguments from both sides would include a number of false promises (which, as we all know, are binding only for those who believe them), but surely not the degree of lying, intolerance and violence which led to the murder of a young MP. This gulf between emotion and reason was reflected in the campaign strategies and slogans adopted by both Leave and Remain.

The analysis and strategy of the Remainers could be summed up by the famous rejoinder of Bill Clinton's adviser during the 1992 Presidential campaign: 'the economy, stupid'. During the last days of the Remain campaign, the premise that the economy was all-important seemed to be accurate. The vital importance of the economy had also impacted the result of the referendum on Scottish independence in October 2014. At the time, uncertainty surrounding whether it would be possible to introduce a currency independent of the Bank of England, together with interventions from business leaders – notably the boss of Waitrose, who explained that the price of goods in supermarkets would be higher in the event of independence – had persuaded those Scots who were hesitant not to take the risk. Therefore, it seemed obvious that no one in a country like the United Kingdom would vote to become poorer. All that was needed was to use some of the same arguments that had worked so well against independence for Scotland. Instructions were given accordingly and figures were published on the anticipated negative economic consequences of Brexit. Top experts were called on to contribute to this exercise: representatives of the City, of employers (CBI), and the Institute of Directors (IOD), as well as the remarkable Governor of the Bank of England Mark Carney. But these forecasts, which could not be verified and were not entirely credible – sometimes because they were over-precise, for example one projection forecast a loss of £4,564 a year for each family – were challenged as a matter of principle, and the whole campaign dismissed by Brexiteers as 'project fear', or scaremongering.

At a certain moment the Brexiteers, aware that they could not win the economic argument, changed tactics and used the issue of immigration to go on the offensive, a topic which the Remain campaign strategists had decided not to engage with, preferring to stick to their chosen course. Whatever the question under discussion, David Cameron continued to repeat the mantra – in a rhythm that still plays in my head – that the UK would be 'stronger, safer and better off' in all respects by staying within the European Union. I watched mind-blowing televised debates where – no matter if he was speaking to people from Nigeria or the Indian subcontinent – he persisted endlessly with this refrain to those who, having acquired British nationality recently themselves, were upset that he was not keeping his promise to end immigration. What's more, this message, like the whole Remain campaign, was far too abstract, too general: it didn't address particular stakeholders or use concrete everyday examples that were directly relevant to his audience.

In the Remain campaign, no other topic was really addressed. When I expressed surprise at this, I was told that the plan was for the campaign to be structured by theme, starting with the economy, then foreign policy in terms of security and influence, followed by the risk of Scotland becoming independent and finally the consequences for the Good Friday Agreement which had ended the conflict in Northern Ireland. These arguments, taken together, were in theory sufficient to demonstrate the harmful effects of Brexit and, at first, the campaign seemed to be proceeding as planned. One morning in May 2016, ambassadors were invited to the symbolic Great Court of the British Museum – 'a museum of the world for the world', to quote former Museum Director Neil MacGregor – to hear a presentation by David Cameron. Cameron was assisted by the talented former Labour Foreign Minister David Miliband, who had come from New York for the occasion. In his speech, the Prime Minister underlined the contribution to peace made by the European Union; the merits of close co-operation with the UK's European partners, in order to meet the challenges of the day (Daesh, Russia, the refugee crisis); and warned against the risk of a lost decade in the event of Brexit. But an article in *The Times,* published that very morning, mocked this altogether sensible presentation, claiming that David Cameron had threatened the catastrophe of World War Three in the event of Brexit. Ridiculed in this way, the Prime Minister simply abandoned the topic instead of explaining it further in the following days with the help of other foreign policy experts. Although there was a well-argued intervention in Chatham House by former Foreign Secretary William Hague who, like his successor Philip Hammond, had switched from being inherently Eurosceptic to become an informed supporter of the EU, based on the well-understood interests of the United Kingdom. When I raised this point with one of the campaign organisers, he replied that it was pointless to pursue the matter further since the British were not interested in foreign policy. End of story. And what about the risk of a renewed demand for Scottish independence? No, it was decided not to speak about this at all on the grounds that credence should not be given to the possibility of a second such referendum. Likewise,

Ireland – which was to become the main bone of contention during negotiations with the European Union – was a non-subject during the campaign.

Another non-subject was the outcome of the earlier negotiation on the reform of the EU. While this four-point reform proposed by London was not revolutionary, it was not insignificant either. The provision that the reference to 'an ever-closer union among the peoples of Europe' in the preamble to the Treaty of Rome would not apply to the United Kingdom, guaranteed that the British would not be bound to closer political integration. Similarly, the assurance that other currencies could exist alongside the euro dispelled the fear that the single currency would impose constraints on the pound. Also, David Cameron succeeded in reducing the amount of family benefits payable by Her Majesty's Government to the children of immigrants, even when they remained in their country of origin. The fact that Europe had been 'reformed' in this way at his request was to have been the argument that would ease his passage from a Eurosceptic – his brand image, especially since his 2013 Bloomberg speech on Britain's relationship with the European Union – to a resolute advocate for remaining in the EU. This speech, which Cameron used to announce the referendum, formed the basis of his EU policy for the weeks, months and years to come – as he promised it would – and as I was able to confirm during my first two years in London. On that day, he bet his political future and initiated the fatal process that he genuinely thought could be avoided.

So, the Prime Minister launched himself into negotiations with the 27, with the aim of achieving a special status for his country. After several months of, sometimes difficult, discussions with the Europeans – who tried to help him without compromising the foundations of the EU – an agreement was reached. However, this agreement was almost immediately consigned to oblivion. No effort was made to educate or to explain the heartfelt reasons for staying in the EU, which instead was presented as the lesser of two evils, whereas leaving was depicted as a leap into unchartered waters. No doubt the best argument, one that David Cameron never really explained properly, was that the United Kingdom had 'the best of both worlds' – it enjoyed all the benefits as part of the biggest trading block in the world while having obtained, over the years and by different prime ministers, various exemptions and a limitation of obligations, notably in relation to the single currency and the Schengen arrangements.

And so, the Government began to tie its own hands. Firstly, as demanded by the Brexiteers, by strictly following the rule of 'purdah' – the Persian and Urdu word for 'curtain' or 'veil' that was adopted into English during the time of the British Raj – meaning that government officials had to stay silent during the campaign. For four weeks, the Government did not use state resources even though they were not obliged to adopt the rule, given that this was a referendum and not a general election. In other words, civil servants were not allowed to do anything that might support the campaign; many of them complained that they were more or less laid off. Secondly, David Cameron agreed to leave the members of his Cabinet at liberty to support or oppose the Remain campaign, which created an extremely unpleasant atmosphere and a real cacophony.

Given the lacklustre campaign, the abstract slogan targeting economic interests alone, and the handicaps that David Cameron had imposed upon himself, it was easy for the leaders of Brexit – in particular Dominic Cummings, the unconventional strategist of the Leave campaign – to focus on a theme and slogan to rally and resonate with those who felt frustrated. This was 'Take Back Control'. But control of what, and how? Apparently this was of little importance. Each person took from the slogan what they wanted: control of their life, having lost out to immigrants accused of taking their job; their hospital bed; their children's place in school; rejection of the globalisation that they deemed responsible for the UK being supposedly dispossessed and left behind. They wanted control of their towns, where they believed too many shops and notices advertised in foreign languages – like the very English town of Rugby in which the tolerance threshold was crossed given that more than 60 per cent of the population was Polish. They wanted control of their country, which they perceived as being subjected to the orders of unelected European officials.

Brexiteers dreamed of turning back the clock and returning to the country of their youth, or that of their parents. Just as the Beatles sang 'I believe in yesterday', so too did Brexiteers yearn for yesterday's world. The British Empire triumphant, the made-up history told to children in *The Story of Our Island,* the everyday heroism of the English in *Dad's Army,* or the beguiling realm of *Downtown Abbey* that fascinated the whole world, including China (some of my friends complained about the 'Downton Abbey effect' on the English people who voted for Brexit inspired by nostalgia and feelings of resentment).

This idea of paradise lost was predominant amongst the Brexiteers' wish list of post-Brexit goals. They wanted to bring back capital punishment, corporal punishment and, most importantly, they wanted the dark blue passport with a cover that would not reference the European Union that they so hated. Theresa May hurried to grant this last wish in 2019, even before the projected departure date, and the Brexiteers celebrated this as a great victory, even though nothing had been preventing them from having a blue passport while still remaining in the EU. There were, of course, sarcastic comments about the fact that these new, purely British, passports were going to be manufactured by a French company, Gemalto, in their Polish factory in Tczew.

To this nostalgia for the past, there was added an underlying hatred for, and distrust in, the establishment – namely politicians and City bankers, who were blamed for the financial crisis of 2008 and its painful and lasting consequences in terms of austerity and unemployment. Well aware of this loss of confidence and hostility, the men of the City remained in the background during the campaign and left it to business leaders to step up to the plate. This rejection of expertise and competence, which affected politicians as well as those in the world of finance, could be seen in the choices of those presenting themselves as anti-establishment; whereas, in fact, they all went to the same schools and, strictly speaking, belonged to the same elite. Populists pretending to speak the language of the people – in an amusing or even buffoon-like fashion in the case of Nigel Farage and Boris Johnson.

It was, therefore, necessary to address two main points of concern, which could be complementary but not necessarily so, and which implied two separate target audiences. On the one hand, there was the problem of identity and the independence of the country; on the other, the fear and rejection of immigration. The first of these concerns had long been a theme dear to the hearts of the few Europhobes in the Tory Party, who were the main, if not only, reason for holding the referendum. They hated the European Union that violated the sacrosanct sovereignty of the Westminster Parliament. It is interesting to note that some ideological Brexiteers of this type appeared not to have a problem with immigration. In fact, one of the most virulent of these Europhobic MPS went so far as to tell me that he was pleased there were Polish workers – more dedicated and competent than their English counterparts – to work on their beautiful homes, and pretty Lithuanian waitresses to serve them in restaurants, rather than grumpy old English ones.

Concerns of independence and identity were of particular relevance to the relatively well-off inhabitants of south-east England, but these concerns also resonated with some farmers, despite the fact that they received numerous subsidies under the Common Agricultural Policy, relied heavily on seasonal workers from the EU, and exported 80 per cent of their produce to the European Union. Indeed, they were among the first to feel the adverse effects of their vote and to bemoan the risk of seeing their harvest rotting in the ground. And what is to be said about Wales and Cornwall? Both showed the same hostility to Brussels, despite being the regions that received the most European subsidies. They actually seemed surprised after the vote that they would be receiving no more.

Identity politics aside, it was the theme of immigration that was at the heart of the Leave campaign, to the extent that it could be said that the referendum had more to do with immigration than with the European Union. It's a well-known fact that a vote of this type is rarely a response to the question actually being asked. France, as I often reminded people, went through this experience with the referendum of 2005 when the electorate rejected a draft 'European Constitution', prepared under the presidency of Valéry Giscard d'Estaing, whereas at the start of the campaign there had been a large majority in favour.

In the UK, particularly England, the target was wider and included the underprivileged and deprived neighbourhoods of the industrial, or de-industrialised, north-east where the Tories had very few supporters and not many sensors either. This lack of Tory representation meant that the Labour Party had been left in charge of the Remain campaign in these regions. The bigger cities of the North, like Manchester and Liverpool – led by committed Labour mayors, whom I had met – would mostly vote to stay in the European Union. But somehow Nigel Farage succeeded in convincing the frustrated inhabitants of suburban housing estates across the north of England that the EU, which had made freedom of movement an absolute obligation, was responsible for the influx of refugees. It mattered little that there were no refugees at all in some areas – it seemed to be enough to scare citizens into siding with Farage. I remember one BBC news report when someone who lived in one of these Northern regions said he was going to vote Brexit because of the number of immigrants in the UK. When the reporter asked if he had ever seen an immigrant, he said no but he knew they were everywhere

What did it matter that there were as many immigrants from developing nations – over whom the UK had total control, given that they were not protected by the EU freedom of movement – as there were European nationals? (The latter, significantly, were categorised as migrants, unlike in continental countries where they are called European citizens.) Or that the United Kingdom, like all EU member states, had the right to send immigrants home if they hadn't found work within three months? This option was used by other European countries but never in the United Kingdom, and that was for two reasons.

The first was that, in order to protect civil liberties and for historical reasons that are no longer relevant in the age of terrorism, the British have always refused to introduce identity cards. After the war, Churchill abolished the ones that had been used during the conflict, judging that they were no longer needed in times of peace. This is somewhat ironic, given that the number of surveillance cameras and DNA databases is certainly higher in the UK today than in other EU countries. It was, therefore, difficult to keep track of illegal immigrants, even if a late attempt was made to dissuade employers, landlords and banks from offering them jobs, accommodation or bank accounts.

The second, and perhaps more significant, reason was that the economy was strong – there was full employment and the booming construction sector in particular needed hard workers. The NHS also needed foreign doctors and nurses since not enough were being trained in Britain. (Even Boris Johnson admitted that there were no longer any English candidates for bus driver vacancies in London.) It is true that 2015 saw record net immigration at around 330,000. In total, more than eight million UK residents – 13 per cent of the population – were born abroad. The speed of this demographic change was unprecedented in the United Kingdom.

It was the year that pressure from Calais was at its highest, with lorries being attacked at the entrance to the tunnel; the time when migrants in the Calais 'Jungle' recharged their mobile phones at the Jules Ferry centre in order to consult job offers in London, where they were told by people smugglers they would be welcomed with open arms. There had also been an explosion in the numbers of migrants arriving in the ports of Lampedusa in Italy and Lesbos in Greece, something which was in the news almost daily.

The report in September 2015 that Angela Merkel was going to welcome nearly one million refugees blocked at the Hungarian border, together with the 'fake news' that these people would inevitably end up in the paradise that was the UK, was exploited with gusto by the tabloid press. It served as a pretext for some months later, less than a week before the referendum, when the disgraceful images emerged of Nigel Farage posing in front of a poster of a queue of refugees crossing the Croatian border on the way to a refugee camp in Slovenia. The poster was entitled *Breaking Point*; the caption read: 'The EU has failed us all. We must break free of the EU and take back control of our borders.' A complaint for incitement to racial hatred was immediately filed by the General Secretary of Unison Dave Prentis – Unison being one of the largest trade unions in the United Kingdom – who said that the militants of Leave had descended into the gutter. Others even felt that the poster resembled Nazi propaganda. It shocked the whole political establishment and even embarrassed Boris Johnson, in charge of the official 'Vote Leave' campaign. He distanced himself from UKIP's openly racist approach, saying that it represented neither his campaign, nor his policy and that he was passionately pro-immigration and pro-migrant. But the damage had been done and, in reality, this whole anti-migrant campaign served the purpose of the Leave leaders who could reap the benefits without getting their own hands dirty.

Another point of contention that suddenly emerged was Turkey. Its membership of the EU was presented as being imminent, with the implication that the United Kingdom would soon be overrun by some 70 million Turks. Minister of State for the Armed Forces Penny Mordaunt had no hesitation in telling the BBC that London would have no choice in the matter as it would not have a right of 'veto'.[1] This was blatantly false since the accession of any new member must be unanimously approved by the EU Council and then ratified by all national parliaments. No mention was made of this or of the fact that, before any accession, Ankara would have to meet all the criteria for adopting the *acquis communautaire* (the EU's body of law), chapter by chapter. Or, that the negotiations that began in 2005, following a request made by Turkey back in 1987, had so far enabled only 16 out of 35 chapters to be discussed, with agreement being reached on only one of them. David Cameron once said that at that rate, Turkey would not be joining before the year 3000.

It was already clear that the nationalistic and Islamic policies being adopted by President Erdoğan were changing minds in most of Europe; the reticence of Paris, and its ability to oppose any such accession were also well-known. But since London's traditional position, encouraged by the United States, was to let Turkey, a member of NATO, join the European Union, no British leader had been willing to take a definitive stance. David Cameron had left the matter open, simply saying that it was not currently relevant, without saying clearly that it would not happen. For his part, Boris Johnson said that Britain had long supported Turkey's membership of the EU without saying when this might occur, thereby helping to maintain a level of fear amongst his compatriots. Secretary of State for Justice Michael Gove added fuel to the fire by asserting that nearly five million Europeans would soon have the right to live and work in the United Kingdom with the forthcoming accession of Albania, Macedonia, Montenegro and Serbia. The initial lie always carries more weight than all the corrections made subsequently by those more concerned with the truth.

The sad truth of the immigration/EU link was that it was most often non-white immigrants who were the subject of concern. I was witness to this several times: myself and journalist James O'Brian constantly heard it in his conversations with his listeners on the Leading Britain's Conversation (LBC) radio channel. Priti Patel used her background to convince a large proportion of people from the Indian subcontinent to vote Leave, against their own interests, by claiming that they could in this way make room for an influx of 'curry chefs' and members of their families, instead of the Polish (sadly detested by much of Britain). The day following the referendum, certain members of this community who paid the price of the ambient xenophobia regretted their vote, considering that they had been misled.

This atmosphere of hatred against the EU and migrants is what led to the tragic murder of Jo Cox on 16 June 2016, who was on her way to a constituency surgery in Birstall, Yorkshire. She was savagely killed by a bullet to the head and several stab wounds as the killer shouted: 'Britain First, keep Britain independent!' It was quickly said to have been the act of a mentally deranged person – no doubt, but he was, above all, a fanatic from the extreme right, acting within an atmosphere so toxic as to encourage such deeds. It brought to mind Ariel's lines in *The Tempest*: 'Hell is empty, and all the devils are here'.[2] However, this travesty did not stop Nigel Farage from claiming afterwards that Brexit had been accomplished without 'a single bullet being fired'. Jo Cox's murder sent shock waves throughout the country. It was perceived as an attack on British democracy and everyone, except UKIP, paused their campaigns for a few days. There was hope that the horror of the crime would calm things down and that reason would prevail. But it was not enough, and the campaigns proceeded, daggers drawn. Reason, pragmatism and self-restraint had all flown the coop.

By making clever use of the internet and all of the personal data of Facebook users fraudulently accessed by Cambridge Analytica it was possible, surreptitiously, to identify people who might be persuaded to vote for Brexit. This company, which counted Steve Bannon – a militant from the American extreme right – amongst its shareholders, played a similar role in the election of Donald Trump. The scandal burst into the open in May 2018 and Cambridge Analytica went bankrupt – although another company, Emerdata, retrieved its data. In this way, the Leave campaign was able to identify people who took no interest in politics; people who were off the radar, or who didn't vote and who were considered, by all political parties, as being hopeless cases and not worth a doorstep visit by campaigners; people who nobody, except Arron Banks, UKIP's financial backer, had even thought of polling. I remember it being said, just before the vote, that if the turnout was high, that would be positive as it would mean that many young people – instinctively pro-Europe for the most part – had come out to vote, but if the turnout was too high, that would be bad as it would mean that people who never usually voted had gone to cast a vote for Brexit. It was the second of these theories that turned out to be the case. In a very striking scene from a BBC telefilm on the run-up to the vote, Benedict Cumberbatch – the cult actor who starred as an off-beat Sherlock Holmes – played to perfection the role of Dominic Cummings paying a visit to a caravan to listen to, and convince, people who had been abandoned by everybody else. Such people had nothing more to lose and were all the more susceptible to the sirens of Brexit because they had the feeling that nobody ever listened to them.

The Leave campaign was characterised by disinformation, invention, manipulation and deliberate lies, including the most outlandish ones such as the claim that the EU would demand the end of the British monarchy – 'They're going to get rid of the Queen' was a common refrain. Given the attachment of the great majority of the UK population to their monarch, there is little doubt that this had an effect. UKIP's brochures had no hesitation in claiming that staying in the EU would mean the end of the Queen and the royal family.

And of course, how can anyone ever forget the emblematic symbol of Brexit? The red bus crisscrossing the country with Boris Johnson aboard proclaiming that the £350 million paid every week to the European Union could henceforth be spent on the health service instead. (A Leninist system that should be privatised, was how one of its liberal critics described it to me one day.) Shortly after taking up my duties, I was invited by the London School of Economics to a roundtable discussion of the Transatlantic Trade and Investment Partnership (TTIP), the free trade agreement being negotiated with the United States. I was astonished to find that some of the British were even more reluctant than the French to sign up to this agreement, which they thought constituted a threat to their NHS.

So busy were they looking for arguments to stir up anger, fear and resentment, that none of the political leaders supporting the Leave campaign took the time to specify what the Brexit project actually was. Most of those who were invited to speak on television insisted that Brexit did not mean leaving the single market or the customs union, few of them really knowing what they were talking about. Winston Churchill was sarcastic about speakers who didn't know what they were going to say when they stood up, when they were speaking didn't know what they were talking about, and when they sat down, didn't know what they had said. As for the jovial Boris Johnson, he kept repeating that Brexit would offer fantastic opportunities. But which ones? He never elaborated and, at the end of the day, no one really asked. That wasn't what it was about. Thus, against all expectations, on 23 June 2016, (disconsolate) emotion triumphed over reason – 51.9 per cent in favour of leaving against 48.1 per cent for remaining.

One MP, an astute analyst of British political life, had assured me that the campaign would be dirty and bumpy but in the end, British pragmatism would win the day and the British would remain in the EU. Dirty and bumpy the campaign certainly was, but in the end, they left.

CHAPTER 5

'Whodunit'? The Guilty Parties

THE DAY FOLLOWING this unforgettable referendum, the first question was – what just happened? Then – what went wrong? After that – why? And lastly, the primary question in any English detective story – whodunit? Many seminars and roundtable discussions were organised in the wake of the result; many articles and books were published on the subject, of which the most explicit as regards identifying the guilty parties was *Guilty Men: Brexit Edition*, published a year later under the nom-de-plume Cato the Younger.[1]

As with Agatha Christie's *Murder on the Orient Express*, there were several guilty parties and accomplices, albeit with different reasons for being involved. There were those in charge, the architects of the campaign, the spokespersons, and those who embellished the arguments. Some played a more decisive role than others but they all delivered a stab wound. Given the narrow margin of victory, it can be said that without each and every one of them, Brexit would not have happened.

Without a doubt, the first guilty party is David Cameron. His name will go down in history as the prime minister who led his country out of the European Union 'by accident', as the now-famous Speaker of the House of Commons John Bercow said to a visiting delegation from the French Parliament a few weeks after the referendum. While his friends George Osborne, a Remain supporter, and Michael Gove, a Eurosceptic (euphemism for Europhobe), had warned him about the risks of such a vote, David Cameron thought that by promising a referendum on the European Union, he could kill two birds with one stone – marginalise the UKIP nationalist party and, most importantly, bring together the Conservative Party, which for decades had been split (poisoned, indeed) by the hatred of Europe on the part of a handful of MPs. Entirely focussed on this goal, he did not take on the Brexiteers in his own party and, in particular, took care not to antagonise Boris Johnson. I remember attending the reception to mark the end of Boris Johnson's term as mayor of London, held in the stunning London Transport Museum in Covent Garden. Surrounded by several generations of London's iconic red buses, the guest of honour, to everyone's surprise, was David Cameron. He gave a speech paying tribute to the man who had betrayed him by choosing to back the Leave campaign, thereby becoming his principal adversary. It was clear to me that day that David Cameron was playing the 'second round', the post-referendum when Boris Johnson would return to the fold.

A Belgian colleague once jokingly said to me that David Cameron was a gambler who, in order to make the game more exciting, replaced Russian roulette with 'Belgian roulette' – a game that can't be won since a cartridge is put into every chamber of the pistol.[i] Was he a man too sure of himself, of his luck? This, at any rate, is how he presented himself to his European counterparts. The fact is that under his leadership, the Conservative Party regained power in 2010, after Tony Blair's three mandates and 13 years of New Labour reigning supreme. The coalition with the Liberal Democrats was pretty much a success and he had won the Scottish referendum, despite the somewhat risky concessions he had made to Edinburgh.

But most importantly, and against all expectations, David Cameron had won an absolute majority in the general election of May 2015, just over a year previously. All the predictions had been for a hung Parliament and therefore a new coalition.

---

[i] In France, the cartoon stereotype of Belgians is that they're not very bright.

On the television broadcasts on the evening of the election, the top constitutional experts that I met – in this country without a (written) constitution – laid out, with relish, their theories on the different possible scenarios – the most likely being a renewal of the coalition with the Lib Dems, whose total collapse came as a complete surprise. In fact, Nick Clegg, their attractive, Europhile leader – a graduate of the College of Europe in Bruges – failed to be re-elected, despite David Cameron's support. He paid the price of reneging on his promise not to increase university tuition fees. Paddy Ashdown, a former leader of the Party, incredulous at the exit polls which predicted a fall from 57 to eight seats said, on television, that he would eat his hat if the results during the night did not improve. A promise that he fulfilled several days later, on television, by eating a hat made out of chocolate – British humour *oblige*. This general election, the first since my arrival in London, confirmed André Maurois' assertion in his book *Les Anglais*, that the results of elections in England were as unpredictable as storms.[2]

The day following, I congratulated one of David Cameron's close collaborators who replied 'Amazing, isn't it?!' This unexpected triumph turned out to be a Pyrrhic victory, however, since Cameron was defeated at the referendum some months later. Had they been in a new coalition, the Lib Dems would probably have opposed the holding of a referendum or would at least have laid down conditions to give Remain a chance of winning it. These may have included giving a vote to European citizens living in the UK, to British residents of countries in the European Union, and to young people from the age of 16 as had been done for the Scottish referendum. All these groups were disenfranchised, despite the fact that Brexit would have a direct impact on their daily lives and their future. David Cameron was convinced he would win by presenting his compatriots with a 'reformed Europe', thanks to the concessions he had obtained from Brussels on certain points of importance to the United Kingdom: a guarantee that the pound would not be penalised by decisions taken by the Eurozone; the non-binding character for the United Kingdom of the provision in the preamble relating to the quest for ever-closer union; a limitation on welfare benefits for new immigrants; and a strengthened role for national parliaments. Even though these concessions fell short of the demands spelled out in the Tory manifesto, David Cameron thought that the agreement reached with the EU on these points would be sufficient.

On this basis, he had pledged to devote himself 'heart and soul' to campaigning for the referendum. He assured François Hollande of this fact, and his other European counterparts also, at the Franco-British summit in Amiens, in March 2016. David Cameron kept his word, but it was difficult for him – for ten years he had been a critic of the European Union and the mouthpiece of the Eurosceptics, then suddenly he became a convincing champion of the EU for the duration of the campaign. And he often created his own battles to fight: the European army, which no one had mentioned up until the Brexit campaign, and which was nowhere near coming into being, as well as protection for the City which, according to some of its representatives, was not something that had been asked of him.

Perplexingly, David Cameron returned triumphant to London from EU Council meeting after EU Council meeting, boasting that he had fought valiantly against the European Union. How could that not give the British people the impression that the EU was an adversary rather than a partner and ally? In his autobiography, David Cameron recognised that the Government should have spoken more positively about the European Union and its benefits for the United Kingdom,[3] but whose fault was that? If it's now too late for his country, perhaps it will serve as a useful lesson for other European leaders. Given the predominance of immigration in the debate, perhaps he should, or could, at least have warned his European counterparts about the risk of losing the referendum if he didn't get a bit more power to block immigration. I raised this point on several occasions but the line from Whitehall was that it would have served no purpose since Angela Merkel had very clearly stated that it was unacceptable. At the Amiens summit, David Cameron said he would win the referendum because 'on balance' the advantages of remaining in the EU outweighed the advantages of leaving. He was assuming the electorate would vote on the basis of reason rather than emotion.

Without doubt, David Cameron could have conducted a better campaign – if he had a better understanding of the electorate. He had remained, to some extent, the Notting Hill Tory – modern, laid-back, almost flippant at times – not much liked by the very conservative wing of the Conservative Party, who were resistant to its modernisation and the adoption of gay marriage in particular, which Cameron always proudly presented as one of his successes. He was also proud of the twofold economic and social liberalism he had brilliantly set out in his speech at the Conservative Party Conference in Manchester in October 2015, at the height of his glory – his best speech, I was told.

The main criticism levelled against David Cameron was that he put the interests of his party above those of his country. By trying to bring on side the 40 or so longstanding and fanatical Europhobes in the Tory Party, he intensified an irreparable divide within it, strengthened the Europhobic camp, and provoked what was almost a civil war in the country. It is true that the British are extremely attached to their two traditional parties, neither of which have changed their names in many years, unlike the French Party of the right which has known several incarnations. In fact, the Tory Party, which dates back to 1834, is the heir to the Tories of the 17th and 18th centuries.

David Cameron announced his resignation on 24th June 2016, saying that he could not be 'the captain that steers our country to its next destination'. On the day of his effective resignation, he was criticised for humming a little song as he turned to enter the door of Number 10 for the last time, forgetting of course that he still had a small microphone attached to his lapel. Some journalists were sure that the tune was the theme song to the *West Wing*, the American series about the corridors of power in the White House. He admitted in his autobiography that he had done this in order to calm his nerves, unsure whether or not the door of Number 10 would open for him.[4]

Relief, indifference, thoughtlessness, off-handedness? I don't think so. At the commemoration of the 100th anniversary of the Battle of the Somme – eight days after the political earthquake – there was a moment when, like all once-powerful men who have lost that power or become lame ducks, he walked alone. It made me think of how, years previously, one of our ministers more or less ignored President Eduard Shevardnadze of Georgia – since he was no longer the all-powerful foreign secretary of the Soviet Union – at a General Assembly of the United Nations. After talking to him for a few minutes and making no effort to hide his boredom, the French minister ostentatiously left to take a seat at the other end of the room with his colleagues. *Sic transit gloria mundi* – thus passes the glory of the world.

I sought David Cameron out to tell him that I was very sorry about what had happened. He replied that he was not worried for himself but for his country. In his last conversation with President Hollande that day, he expressed the hope that relations between the United Kingdom and the European Union would change as little as possible – a soft Brexit. But his words no longer carried any weight. Since then, he has remained in the background, writing his memoirs in a shed at the bottom of his garden. (They were published in October 2019 to general indifference.) He also gave up his seat as a MP and 'forgot' to ask for his Westminster access badge to be renewed. History will surely not be kind to him – for angry Remainers, he was an even worse prime minister than Chamberlain, the gold standard in this domain.

David Cameron was the one who pulled the trigger, but Nigel Farage played an important role, even if no doubt more or less confined to his traditional supporters. More than three million of them all the same.

Farage had been preparing for this result for years, even if his party, by reason of the first-past-the-post system, was not winning any seats. He himself, having failed on seven occasions to be elected to Westminster, fell back on the European Parliament – which operated a system of proportional representation – and used this platform to conduct his campaign and insult European institutions and leaders. But he had the stroke of genius to casually claim a link between the European Union, which annoyed the British a little, and massive immigration, which was the foremost concern for much of the population. His banter and pints of beer brandished in public proved popular; his slogans were punchy. His campaign poster *Breaking Point* hit the mark. There is an obvious debt here to the 'Rivers of Blood' speech delivered in April 1968 by Enoch Powell – writer and Conservative Party member hostile to immigration – warning against the apparent dangers of welcoming huge numbers of non-white immigrants from the Commonwealth. This speech was well received by a large proportion of the population but also obviously sparked angry criticism and an anti-racist backlash. Immigration was the dominant theme of Farage's campaign, to the mood music of 'They are taking your jobs, your hospital beds and the places of your children in school.' Despite the over-optimistic vision of an open and tolerant Great Britain, this undercurrent of xenophobia that existed in Enoch Powell's day has not gone away – it had perhaps just stayed under the radar.

Everyone knew what Nigel Farage's position was. But he alone would not have been able to persuade a great many voters of the merits of Brexit. Without the popular Boris Johnson to give it legitimacy, Brexit would probably never have happened. And indeed when David Cameron heard that Boris Johnson was going to refuse to join him in his campaign and promote Brexit instead, he realised full well the danger. Boris Johnson himself admitted that he had hesitated, turning around in his flat like a supermarket trolley and preparing two contradictory speeches. One for remaining in the European Union, the other for leaving.

It was obvious to everyone that his decision was based, purely and simply, on opportunism. His plan was presumably to be able to claim the Tory leadership, and subsequently the prime minister-ship. In a debate during the campaign about the consequences of Brexit in terms of figures, then Secretary of State for Energy and Climate Change Amber Rudd hit the mark when she said that the only figure that really interested Boris Johnson was Number 10. His ambition to be compared to Winston Churchill was evident in his biography of the great leader – not always rigorous, according to historians – where he traces an obvious parallel with his own self, emphasising the human factor, the strength of a man... the strength of a man alone.

Boris – everyone affectionately called him by his first name. Mayor of a world city, in a country where not taking oneself seri-ously is appreciated to such an extent that no one is afraid to appear ridiculous. One of the unforgettable images of Boris as mayor of London saw him dangling for several long minutes from the tangled cable of a zip-line above Victoria Park, waving two small British flags. He was once, without doubt, the most popular and amusing politician in the United Kingdom. An exceptional personality, claiming to have Turkish, Russian and French blood in his veins.

Born in New York, Boris also had American citizenship, which he only gave up in 2015 in order to avoid paying US taxes. His family is one belonging to 'the establishment' and, like his sister Rachel – who is intelligent, bubbly, warm; a journalist, column-ist and novelist – has solid European convictions. His father, the patriarch, Stanley Johnson, whom I met at dinners and the theatre, is a former journalist and European civil servant, a trailblazer on environmental issues, and a strong personality also fond of prov-ocation. Boris has a brother Max, not involved much in politics, and also Jo, whom I saw in various ministerial incarnations, as discreet and professionally rigorous as Boris can be impetuous and vague. An excellent French speaker, Jo had accepted the invitation to be guest of honour at the '*Journée de la francophonie*' at the

French Residence in March 2016, where he gave a pro-European speech. But later, in November 2018, when he was minister of state for transport, he resigned from the May Cabinet in protest against the 'travesty' of the negotiations being conducted by the Prime Minister that would leave the country trapped in a relation of 'vassalage' to the EU. Contrary to his earlier beliefs, for some weeks he joined his brother's Cabinet to promote a hard Brexit. Family loyalty – solidarity of the clan. But Jo's personal convictions prevailed in the end, and he left the Cabinet when Boris unceremoniously expelled 21 respectable Tories from the Conservative Party, who had been members for decades, including Nicolas Soames, the grandson of Winston Churchill.

Like everyone else, I appreciated Boris for his extensive knowledge of the classics, his eccentricity and his ability at all times to make people laugh, including at himself. I was grateful for the solidarity he demonstrated at the time of the terrorist attacks in France. He decided to light up London's main attractions, including London Bridge and Trafalgar Square, in the colours of the French flag in homage to the victims of the *Charlie Hebdo* shootings. He also spontaneously attended a friendly match between France and England after the Nice attack. We were in the same row and he sang 'La Marseillaise' at the top of his voice – he loves speaking French.

But Boris – nicknamed BoJo, then for a while BoGo when he opted for leaving the European Union, or Bozo the clown by this opponents – is also the man who insults the European Union and its members, including the French whom he did not hesitate to call 'turds'.

He is, above all else, an unrepentant liar. As well as being fired after a year from his job with *The Times* for falsifying a quote, and when taken on by *The Daily Telegraph* as its Brussels correspondent, he delighted in making up stories, for instance about the supposed obligation under European law to have straight bananas, rather than curved ones. This led the authors of the little Ladybird book on *The Story of Brexit* to say that it was terribly complicated to be in the European Union and also to leave it,[5] but luckily the question posed in the referendum didn't seem to be complicated at all – 'it was something about the freedom of bananas'. There are countless other examples, just as silly.

But nothing in his background showed him to be anti-immigrant. The first time I met Boris – because that's what everyone calls him, even his opponents, and bizarrely, even on first meeting – a week after arriving in London, I was sat next to him at one of those breakfast meetings so popular with the British. He was the guest of honour and gave a brilliant speech comparing Sparta – a closed and xenophobic city that had disappeared from the map – to Athens, an open city that had survived. He was speaking about London, and thus expressing opinions very far from those of Nigel Farage.

His lies, provocations and insults are effectively legion. When – counter-intuitively – he was appointed as foreign secretary by Theresa May, journalists listed all the, often graphic, insults he had levelled against this or that country or leader. He ended up admitting that it would take a lifetime to apologise to all of them, so he wasn't going to waste his time on doing that.

Boris again proved he was an inveterate liar by tweeting, on the day of the municipal elections of May 2019, that he had just voted Conservative, calling on others to do likewise. The problem is, there were no elections in London that day! A lie to embellish the truth; a lie used to play a game but also used as an instrument of power. The end justifies the means: Boris Johnson considers he is not subject to the same rules as everyone else. Three years after the referendum, the case was brought by the pro-European activist Gina Miller to annul the Prime Minister's decision to prorogue Parliament in September 2019 for three weeks so as to avoid debate and objections. It was founded on the claim that the Prime Minister had lied to the Queen about the reasons for his decision, which he had presented as being obligatory if a new session of Parliament was to be opened.

Boris, no doubt, felt that the fact of belonging as he did to the 'caste' of former pupils of Eton and Oxford entitled him to use inappropriate language and make provocative statements. People will remember his 'Go whistle' in response to the European Union's statement of what the United Kingdom was due financially, but also Michel Barnier's apt retort that he couldn't hear any whistle, just the ticking of the clock counting down the little time there was left for the negotiations. As Boris is nothing if not consistent, he said to me once in French at a dinner – *Vous n'aurez pas un sou, pas un sou* ('You won't get a penny, not a penny'). Asked about the consequences of Brexit for trade, his glib reply was always that the British would continue to buy Italian prosecco, German cars and French cheese. He was surprised when the Italians and Germans retorted that they would prefer to stop selling to one country and continue selling to 27 others.

As an unlikely foreign secretary – described as akin to having Falstaff in Palmerston's office – his blunders will be long remembered also. On an official visit to Myanmar, he decided to recite a poem by Kipling, with distinctly colonialist overtones, in the great Shwedagon Pagoda in Yangon while Her Majesty's Ambassador tried desperately to whisper that it was inappropriate.

The first break from the indulgence customarily shown him occurred the day after Brexit, however, when he was booed on coming out of his house, head bowed, by a crowd of mostly pro-European young Londoners who felt betrayed by their mayor. Then on 14 July 2016, shortly before his appointment as prime minister and three weeks after the referendum, the speech he gave in the gardens of the French Embassy for Bastille Day was also met with boos, which got louder and louder as he continued to speak. (Some British journalists who arrived late told me that they would have booed him too.) 'Angry Remainers' Boris said to me as he was leaving, 'everything will be fine'. He was genuinely surprised when I replied that, on the contrary, I thought that it would be very difficult. At the request of the Foreign Office, there had been no television cameras present but the journalists who had received an official invitation lost no time in sending their own recordings to the television channels. Some days later when I was being interviewed on Sky News, I was jokingly asked if I knew who had been booing. I replied that I didn't know but that 80 per cent of my guests that day were British....

I remember another episode of his fall from grace. On 5 November of Brexit year, his sister Rachel invited me to an evening at her home for a Guy Fawkes Night party. On that day, an effigy of the most unpopular person of the year is burnt on a bonfire. All the neighbouring families gathered in the communal gardens shared by several Notting Hill houses; Rachel arrived a little late, just in time to see a mass of blond hair going up in flames and, somewhat surprised, she asked me if it was the Queen. It was her brother.

Theresa May, whom Boris openly scorned, persisted in keeping him in the Cabinet thinking that he was less dangerous inside than out. She occasionally called him into line but he showed himself to be disloyal and ended up resigning, with David Davies, after a meeting at Chequers, the prime minister's country residence, on 6 July 2018. Theresa May had convened the members of her Cabinet in order to work out a compromise text on Brexit – she had warned that those who refused to sign up to this text would have to order a taxi. The two men did agree to it so as to be able to return in their official cars but resigned the very next day. Boris Johnson, hoping that his time would come, then continued to rail against the 'Remoaners', censure those who didn't have faith in the United Kingdom – 'the greatest country on earth' – and never stopped referring to the 'fantastic opportunities' provided by Brexit, without ever going into detail on what these opportunities were exactly. He fulfilled his dream of becoming prime minister three years after the referendum. In history books, it is certain that he will always be associated with the famous red bus and its £350 million painted on the side. For the rest, we will have to wait and see.

By a stroke of bad luck, like a bolt out of the blue and welcomed with joy by the Conservatives, Jeremy Corbyn was elected
leader of the Labour Party in September 2015 by young people
inspired by his non-conformist style and his ideas from the far
left (some Conservative MPS told me that their children had even
joined this movement). He was a left-winger in the mould of the
1970s – as reflected in his dress sense – who had rarely conformed
to his Party's instructions, having voted against them no less than
148 times. He was the antithesis of Tony Blair's New Labour and
of the centrists who were standing against him: the talented Andy
Burnham, later elected as mayor of Greater Manchester in 2017;
Yvette Cooper, courageous and determined, who used her acer-
bic debating skills to continue the campaign, intervening later in
Parliament to question the Government on the economic impact
of Brexit; Liz Kendall; or Chuka Umunna, the 'British Barack
Obama' – a young and talented lawyer with African and Irish
roots. All were swept aside. Chuka Umunna continued to speak
out against Brexit, but he later left the Labour Party, feeling he
could no longer support its policies.

In 2015, it was not necessary to be a member of the Labour
Party in order to be able to vote for its leader – it was sufficient to
pay a one-off fee of three pounds, an option which was later found
to have been taken up by some 500,000 people (many of whom
did not belong to a traditional political party but to a movement
called Momentum). Jeremy Corbyn is the British Bernie Sanders,
or Jean-Luc Mélenchon and he stands out from the crowd in a
country that apparently supports free trade and liberalism. But
then the same causes seem to be producing the same effects, on
the right or the left, in this period of populism being experienced
by many countries.

It is said that unlike the Conservative Party, in which authori-
tarianism and absolutism are tempered by patricide, Labour does
not usually push its leaders off a cliff. But in this case, moderate members of the Labour Party tried time and again to over-
throw Jeremy Corbyn. The Labour MPS, smelling success, tabled

a motion of no confidence against him less than a month after the referendum, giving rise to resignations on a grand scale. The motion was carried by 170 votes to 40 but Corbyn, first of all, refused to resign and was then re-elected. He remained well-protected by his electoral base and managed to save his skin each time, helped by the fact that the members of the party were no longer able to find a candidate of sufficient standing to put up against him. After several unsuccessful attempts, they gave up and withdrew from the fray.

Ironically, as he had so many times voted against his own party, Jeremy Corbyn did not allow free votes. He demanded iron discipline from his troops and an obedience *perinde ac cadaver* in accordance with the principle of Ignatius of Loyola. More seriously, MPS who didn't toe the party line were tracked down and, in some cases, even received insults and death threats from his supporters, some with antisemitic connotations (this was the fate of a young, Jewish, female journalist Emma Barnett, who was not particularly indulgent during an interview in which Corbyn performed badly, in May 2017, and who afterwards received many abusive tweets branding her as a Zionist shill and a Miss Piggy).[6] This remained a flaw in the party, as support of the Palestinians from some of Corbyn's followers had evolved into veritable antisemitism which he refused to condemn in clear terms. This was arguably evidenced by the indulgence he showed to the former mayor of London, Ken Livingstone – nicknamed Ken the Red – who Corbyn refused to expel, despite him being openly antisemitic.

One the other hand, if Jeremy Corbyn fell out with anyone, he did not hesitate to eliminate even close collaborators, including Hilary Benn, the son of his mentor, Tony the red millionaire. Benn was a true democrat and committed European, an excellent orator who tried to persuade Corbyn, during the campaign, to come out clearly in favour of remaining in the European Union. Benn ended up chairing the Parliamentary Committee on Exiting the European Union, where he formulated and reformulated incisive questions challenging the lack of clarity and contradictions of members of the Government, notably as regards the economic consequences of Brexit. In September 2019, he drafted a Bill designed to make it impossible for the UK to leave the European Union without an agreement.

Corbyn's faithful lieutenant, Shadow Chancellor of the Exchequer John McDonnell – a dyed-in-the-wool Marxist who brandished Mao's Little Red Book on television one day, much to Theresa May's amusement – was the other bogeyman of the party. Given Labour's devastating experience in Scotland where the party's leaders, alongside the Conservatives, had campaigned against independence and lost all their seats to the Scottish National Party (SNP), Corbyn did not engage with the referendum campaign. Instead, this was a task left to Alan Johnson, a competent and highly respected senior Labour politician, but one who did not have his leader's blessing. Other figures from the left, General Secretary of the Trades Union Congress Frances O'Grady, and Mayor of London Sadiq Khan, did what they could with stirring speeches warning workers against the risks of losing the protections they enjoyed under the European Union. At the end of the day, although two-thirds of Labour supporters did vote Remain, it was in the Labour bastions of the North – the 'red wall' – that the greatest number of Leave votes was recorded. What had been considered at best as ambiguity and at worst – and much closer to the truth – as hostility towards the European Union on the part of the Labour leader, had prevented a massive vote to Remain by Labour supporters. Like Boris Johnson, Jeremy Corbyn essentially had his eye on getting into Downing Street and, in the interim, on remaining at the head of his party. He therefore wielded the knife and bears heavy responsibility for the failure of the referendum.

So much for the men, let's now look at the institutions of the United Kingdom. First – the BBC. The position adopted by the Beeb, another sacred cow and model admired throughout the world – the most striking incarnation of British soft power – enraged Remainers. One evening, I asked a young journalist who had welcomed me to Portland Place, the headquarters of the BBC, what he thought about the referendum. He replied that clearly it was unthinkable to even consider leaving the EU. Unlike the written media, the BBC is financially dependent on a licence fee, thereby making it a public service. It is strictly monitored by a government that regards it with suspicion of being a ragbag of left-wingers. It doesn't fear the Government alone, but also the ire and vindictiveness of the *Daily Mail*, which is much more dangerous for the career of BBC journalists and the future of the channel than the columnists of *The Guardian* are. That is why the BBC is constantly in a dilemma. In 2015, just before the general election, an eminent BBC journalist relayed his personal feelings about the outcome with this telling phrase: 'if the Conservatives win, I'll lose my job; if Labour wins, I'll lose my salary.'

The BBC went to absurd lengths to anxiously demonstrate strict impartiality. As a counterweight to the most widely acclaimed experts, it went in search of illustrious nobodies who, according to the Lacanian formula, were self-appointed experts. For example, as sparring partners in debates with former secretaries-general of NATO, heads of information services or chiefs of staff warning about the risk of isolation in the field of security, the BBC invited people whose only qualification was that they were Brexiteers. What they said on the *Today Programme* or during the *Andrew Marr Show* – high-quality broadcasts that set the tone for the day in the case of the former, or the week in the case of the latter – was generally taken at face value. Forgotten was the golden rule of 'check three times', admired by professionals the world over. Rightly or wrongly, the BBC ended up being nicknamed the 'Brexit Broadcasting Corporation.'

The second major institution, the written press – in this country of 12 major newspapers – still had a decisive influence in 2015 and 2016 and it was expected that editorials would come down on one side or the other. The press were divided: *Financial Times*, *The Times*, *The Guardian* and, for the tabloids, *The Daily Mirror*, were pro-Remain; however, the owners of several newspapers hedged their bets, such as the Rothermere family whose *Daily Mail* was fiercely pro-Brexit while the *Mail on Sunday* advocated the status quo. The situation was similar, although the other way round, for Murdoch since unlike *The Times*, *The Sunday Times* was pro-Leave, as was the tabloid *The Sun*.

The United Kingdom is unique in that it has top-quality newspapers – amongst the best and most professional on the planet, with readers throughout the world – existing alongside the famous tabloids, which are now often referred to as the gutter press. The tabloids use sensational headlines, playing upon readers' fears, particularly regarding immigrants. Arguably, the only widely respected newspaper that came out in favour of Brexit was *The Daily Telegraph*, the right-wing paper that employed an author of mendacious articles on the EU, a certain Boris Johnson, as its correspondent in Brussels. (It was also the paper that published his column in favour of Brexit.) The tabloids (with the exception of *The Daily Mirror*, as mentioned above) opted for Leave. The *Daily Mail*, the newspaper of 'Middle England' is deserving of special mention: this paper, which sells more than one million copies every day and has the most widely read website in the world, has enormous influence and was the Brexit paper *par excellence*. For a long time before the Brexit referendum, the *Daily Mail* had vilified the Brussels elite and formed public opinion against Europe – while the Remain campaign was only a few months old by June 2016, the campaign for Brexit had in fact begun several years previously in the tabloids.

This period of the early 2010s coincided with a sharp rise in the popularity of social media, combined with the fraudulent use of data by Cambridge Analytica. In the old days, pubs served as the meeting place where disconsolate neighbours could come together to grumble. The online world has now become a huge pub where everyone can 'have a go', complain, insult and threaten with complete impunity, protected as they are by anonymity – there is a consensus of, 'since many think like me, I must be right.'

And us? Did the European Union act in good faith? Has it examined its own conscience? During a period of change when the migrant issue affected all our countries, could we have shown more flexibility in relation to the United Kingdom? Could the EU have played a more positive role instead of holding back, paralysed, not even taking the trouble to correct the obvious lies told by the partisans of Brexit? Accused of over-regulating and being too bureaucratic, it simply confined itself to not add fuel to the flames in the run-up to the referendum. But the Europeans had evolved in Paris as in Berlin: the project of increasing federalism had given way to an intergovernmental, more flexible approach based on concentric circles. Migration had become a problem for everyone – in the United Kingdom, the immigration in theory being challenged was intra-EU, whereas in the other member states it concerned developing countries which were experiencing economic or political difficulties. Sooner or later, it would have been necessary to adopt a truly European policy on migration.

But the Europeans were tired of continually having to accord special status to the British. And David Cameron himself had asked them to keep a low profile, to not interfere in UK domestic policies, for fear of upsetting the Eurosceptics. It's difficult to help someone who doesn't want your help. Did Angela Merkel make a big mistake in welcoming lock, stock and barrel nearly one million refugees? Or especially in telling the British that no flexibility on the issue of free movement was possible, given that the four freedoms (movement of goods, services, capital and persons) were intangible and indivisible?

It's hard to reply to these questions, but the paradox is that the necessary reforms to the European Union could have been carried out from the inside with the active participation of the United Kingdom. The second paradox is that the EU will no doubt be reformed in the way advocated by the British – introducing more flexibility – but without them.

CHAPTER 6

The Day – Days, Weeks, Months, Years – After

FOR THOSE WHO had gone peacefully to bed the night before, waking up on the morning of 24 June 2016 was a shock. Incredulity. Shock and incredulity on the part of those who had lost, but also those who had won. (During the night, 80 MPs had written a letter of support to the Prime Minister.) Even when informing David Cameron that he was going to campaign for Leave, Boris Johnson told him that Brexit 'won't happen' – he kept repeating this in private right up until the day before the referendum.

In the ministries of Whitehall in London, as elsewhere, people looked at each other in disbelief. An official from the Ministry of Justice said, in bewilderment, to one of my colleagues: 'We know we have hit an iceberg but we don't know anything more than that'. For Remain supporters, it was like the announcement of a divorce or bereavement and was often accompanied by some form of denial – something had been snatched away from them. Some even admitted to crying; anger came next. There was also very often a feeling of shame for a vote perceived as being retrograde and xenophobic. People even apologised to me on several occasions – at least ten times. One example was at the *Financial Times* summer party which was held a few days after the vote. Among the stories I heard was that of a young Frenchman who had celebrated his birthday – a little noisily – on the evening of the referendum. The next morning, he saw his neighbour hurrying towards him and, somewhat embarrassed and expecting her to complain, he got ready to say sorry. He was extremely surprised when, instead, she apologised profusely for the Brexit vote.

The certainties of the 3.7 million European nationals who had lived happily in London for years and considered it home, evaporated overnight. Many that I spoke with shared the heartfelt sentiment: 'On 23rd June we were Londoners, on the 24th we became foreigners'. There was a strong feeling of injustice since they had not been allowed to vote, unlike any citizen of the Commonwealth – no matter how recently they arrived. From the outset, they were afraid of being bargaining chips in the negotiations. In fact, their situation had not been settled. Some, in particular from the Polish community, returned to their home country, as did many French; others began the process of obtaining British nationality or permanent residency. But the feeling of bitterness remains. As for the fate of the million-and-a-half British citizens settled in EU countries – perfectly integrated into local life, in some cases municipal counsellors – as far as Brexit supporters were concerned, this was the least of their worries.

On the morning of 24 June, the atmosphere changed in London and the rest of the country. Demons had been let loose, and taboos broken – things that used to be kept as private inner thoughts, or were said between friends or neighbours in the pub after a beer or two, had been validated by a victory that seemed to legitimise intolerance, hatred and xenophobia. People of colour were the target of exacerbated racism. The day after the referendum result, insults against foreigners could be heard on the street, or on the tube: 'Go back to your own country! That's what we voted for.' No one was safe. My Swedish counterpart, unused to having her compatriots treated in this manner, was particularly shocked. The Poles were in the front line, and insulting graffiti against 'Polish vermin' was daubed on the walls of the Polish Cultural Institute. This outpouring of hate culminated in physical attacks against members of the Polish community, one of which – in August, in the new town of Harlow, not far from London – proved fatal.

The French Embassy and Consulate General organised meetings with French Consulate advisers to keep a record of such verbal aggressions. Reports were many and varied: one charming young businesswoman with two small, well-behaved children was roundly criticised on the tube for daring to speak French. The French were often accused of cowardice and told to go back to their own country where they were promised the same fate as befell them during the Second World War.

Many Londoners said they no longer recognised their country which they thought, rightly or wrongly, had a reputation for tolerance and moderation. Alarmed by these excesses, MPS launched a campaign against hate crime called 'Better Than That'; I, along with several other ambassadors, was invited to the launch ceremony at Westminster. I was also invited to give evidence of verbal aggressions to a House of Commons committee. In a parallel initiative, the recently-elected mayor of London, Sadiq Khan, took active measures against the onslaught of abuse. Along with the ambassadors of the predominant foreign communities in London, I was invited to City Hall where he warmly reassured us all that London would remain an open city where the rights and safety of foreigners would be protected, and encouraged us to report any physical or verbal attacks to Scotland Yard. The friendly and affable Permanent Under-Secretary at the Foreign and Commonwealth Office Simon McDonald together with a representative of the Home Office, also invited the ambassadors of the EU 27 in order to assure us that the rights of our compatriots would be respected.

Yet, the abuse didn't stop; instances of it, at times surreal, increased. One day in the street, a woman was ordered, by an enraged passer-by, to speak English. (This happened in Wales and the woman in question had been speaking Welsh, the national language.) European partners of UK citizens who had lived in the country for 20 or 30 years and whose children were British by birth received letters from the Home Office – their application for British nationality or right of residence had been judged inadmissible.

Nearly two years later, the so-called Windrush scandal in April 2018 showed more abhorrent abuse that immigrants and their descendants faced in the UK. The people concerned in this instance were Jamaicans, the first 492-strong contingent of whom arrived in 1948 on board the ship *Empire Windrush*. They had been invited to come to work in the United Kingdom, which was lacking in manpower, to help reconstruct the country after the Second World War. Hundreds of thousands of others from the Caribbean arrived subsequently, and perfectly legally, up until 1973. These people, as 'Citizens of the United Kingdom and Colonies' enjoyed an automatic right of residence in the UK. But no documents were issued at the time and the only written proof they had of their right to live in the country was their certificate of passage on the boats; however, one day, these certificates were, purely and simply, destroyed by the Home Office. After the Home Secretary had decided to create a hostile environment for immigrants, 50,000 of the 'Windrush generation', including their descendants, found themselves in an irregular situation from one day to the next, incapable of proving their right of residence in a country without identity cards, deported, incarcerated or refused the right to return if they left to visit family abroad. The Home Secretary Amber Rudd was obliged to resign in April 2018 as a result of this scandal, even though it was not her doing. But that didn't solve the problem completely, even if Theresa May did issue an apology and assure the persons concerned that they could remain in Britain, as they had been promised on their arrival.

* * *

The political burlesque show began the day after the referendum and has continued ever since – it reminded me of *House of Cards*. It is often forgotten that the first, so deliciously British 1990's version of this BBC series on obsession with power, ambition, intrigues, betrayal, vengeance and cynicism – which I so much enjoyed watching in my sitting room in Kensington Palace Gardens – was every bit as good as the better-known American remake.

The procedure for selecting a new Tory leader is well established. It is for the all-powerful 1922 Committee comprising 18 Conservative backbenchers – nicknamed the 'men in grey suits', even though the committee now includes some female members – to oversee the process that starts with several eliminatory rounds of voting by Tory MPS.[i] The 160,000 or so members of the Conservative Party are then invited to choose between the two candidates who received the most votes. The 1922 Committee has the power of life and death over a Tory leader's career. It can convoke the prime minister at any time in order to tell them that they have lost the confidence of the party and thus must resign. Margaret Thatcher had the bitter experience of being betrayed by her own colleagues in this way in November 1990, before it was the turn of Theresa May in May 2019.

When David Cameron resigned as prime minister, everyone thought that Boris Johnson, Brexit's key protagonist, was the obvious next candidate and would win the contest. He was due to make an appearance on television at the end of June 2016 and everyone was expecting him to announce that he was running for the post. But to general astonishment, towards the end of a short speech, he said that he could not be the next prime minister. (It would be as if, in the elections that followed in the United States, Donald Trump changed his mind and renounced the presidency after his victory.) Logically, the second favourite seemed to be the Secretary of State for Justice Michael Gove, who had worked in tandem with Boris Johnson during the campaign but who, by suddenly withdrawing his support for Johnson – saying that he was not fit for the job of prime minister – donned the mantle of traitor and was therefore eliminated, sabotaging his own chances. Then, everyone was expecting a contest during the summer between

---

[i] A parliamentary group of Conservative backbenchers set up after the general election of 1922, triggered by the withdrawal of the Tories from the Government of David Lloyd George.

two women – Minister of State at the Department of Energy and Climate Change Andrea Leadsom, and Home Secretary Theresa May. The next twist in the saga came the following weekend when Andrea Leadsom gave an interview to *The Sunday Times* claiming that, being a mother with therefore a very real stake in the future of the country, she would make a better prime minister than Theresa May who didn't have children.[1] Being a mother had, moreover, been the principal argument of her campaign in favour of Brexit. The bad taste and cruelty of such a remark – knowing that Theresa May had already expressed her regret at not having been able to have children – led to such a public outcry, even from senior members of her own party, that she in turn had to withdraw. I remember watching her withdrawal statement on television on a late Monday morning in the Ambassadors' Entrance in the Foreign Office before attending a meeting with the Permanent Secretary to hear about the UK's plans for the future of European citizens. While waiting for a young official to come and fetch us, I watched with three of my counterparts – incredulous, fascinated and close to laughter – this latest disconcerting episode in what was to be the long saga of Brexit.

So that left Theresa May – 'the only adult in the room', as the saying goes. Her nomination, after the other candidates had been eliminated, was greeted by everyone with relief. The United Kingdom, which had just lived through a moment of incredible folly, seemed to be back on track. It was not a Brexiteer who won, not a 'revolutionary' like her three rivals, but a conservative with a small 'c' who was perceived, rather, as a Remainer, albeit a lukewarm one. Remain supporters accused her of keeping her head below the parapet during the campaign; nevertheless, belonging to the Remain camp no doubt impelled her to become more of a royalist than the king.

Elected by 329 MPs, without the need for any vote by party members, far less the wider electorate, Theresa May became leader of the Conservative Party, then prime minister on 13 July 2016, three weeks after the referendum. the Father of the House of Commons Kenneth Clarke, a man of strong convictions and a wicked sense of humour, seemed to have done her a favour by confiding to the BBC – thinking he was off air but, in fact, with his microphone still connected – that she was 'a safe pair of hands' but 'a bloody difficult woman'. She took this as a compliment saying that the first person who would discover this character trait was the President of the Commission Jean-Claude Juncker, a man much detested in the United Kingdom.

I met Theresa May several times in her premiership and then regularly with her French counterpart Bernard Cazeneuve (with whom she enjoyed a good working relationship, and indeed friendship). Working together, they reached a compromise on Calais in August the year before when they visited to sign an agreement on strengthening security (which included a financial contribution from the United Kingdom and a promise to take in some refugee children). I went with them in a helicopter from Paris to Calais and the understanding between them was obvious. The hot topic of the day, apart from the migration problem in Calais, was the incredible breakthrough made by the left-wing radical, Jeremy Corbyn, who had just won the Labour Party leadership contest. It was also Theresa May who represented the UK government at the French Embassy to observe a minute's silence after the terrorist attack against *Charlie Hebdo*, and we were invited to appear together on the *Andrew Marr Show* to comment on the Bataclan attacks. Side by side, we listened to the Marseillaise sung, in homage to our dead, by a tenor from the Royal Opera Covent Garden.

In my personal experience, she was a sincere, reliable, honest and touching woman. This last adjective may seem surprising to those who have so often seen her as 'Maybot', repeating mindless slogans over and over again like a robot. But I remember a small dinner at the French Residence when she told Bernard Cazeneuve about her political vocation and career, her dream since the age of 13 to become an MP at Westminster. She was also discreetly feminist, appointing and promoting women within her ministry. How did she end up falling into disgrace and being considered 'the worst prime minister ever', at least until the arrival of her successor? Her rigour became stubbornness and mental rigidity. To succeed in implementing Brexit against all the odds and even against the economic interests of her country became her 'sacred mission'. This is the term she used herself, which gave rise to condescending comments about her 'vicar's daughter complex'.

During her time as prime minister, she was shy, often awkward, uncomfortable about displaying any feelings or emotion publicly, something she was criticised for after the tragic fire in June 2017 at Grenfell Tower in North Kensington, a deprived enclave in the upmarket area of Kensington and Chelsea where the French Residence is located. After the death of some 80 people (due to the use of cladding that was unsuitable given the height of the building), Theresa May arrived – late – on the scene but only to thank the firemen. She avoided meeting the families concerned, whereas the Queen had visited the day before to express her compassion.

Wary of trusting others, she isolated herself at the centre of power, delegating everything to two people who became known as the 'gatekeepers' – Fiona Hill, a former Remainer from Scotland who was enjoyable company when off duty, and Nick Timothy, a staunch Brexiteer and ideologue with a Rasputin-type beard and look in his eye, but a supporter of a more social policy. They were the ones who, in their no-nonsense style, relayed the instructions of the Prime Minister – or at times their own – to the members of the Cabinet. Business leaders that I met complained that, unlike David Cameron, Theresa May did not invite them to Downing Street.

However, Theresa May did have her moment of glory – jubilation even – at the first Conservative Party Conference in Birmingham after her election in October 2016 when she appeared triumphant and radiant in an elegant red dress, with her husband at her side. The audience was euphoric, even ecstatic – including my young neighbours in the mezzanine – having been warmed up by Ruth Davidson, the leader of the Tories in Scotland and then rising star, who had succeeded in taking votes from Labour and from Nicola Sturgeon's SNP. For Theresa May, it was the fulfilment of a lifetime dream. Ovations in the hall; the time of the Brexiteers had arrived.

This first combative speech in such a supercharged atmosphere gave the impression that all had been won, that Brexit was the choice of the whole nation and that everyone was heading towards a bright tomorrow. I was accompanied by a brilliant analyst of the legal and institutional subtleties of British political life, Claire Legras, who was responsible for domestic policy at the Embassy. We felt that day that, as far as those in the hall were concerned, the rest of the United Kingdom, the European Union, the world, didn't exist. The Brexiteers were in their element, conversing with each other. Once again, the politicians acted as though they were alone with the most militant of their supporters, all singing from the same hymn sheet, forgetting that there were also journalists present as well as a few ambassadors, invited as observers. They were perhaps not seen as important, but they did, nevertheless, hear the hostile remarks being made about foreigners.

This populist tone of Theresa May's speech was marked, and it shocked also in its condemnation of 'citizens of nowhere', explicitly targeting the urban and cosmopolitan elite – 'If you believe you are a citizen of the world, you are a citizen of nowhere'. On the same day, the new Home Secretary Amber Rudd made a controversial proposal that businesses should be obliged to disclose how many foreigners they employed. The day following this aggressive speech by the Prime Minister, announcing the date of withdrawal from the European Union and seeming to imply that the UK was heading towards a hard and precipitate Brexit, the pound sterling fell to its lowest level against the dollar for 31 years, and the lowest against the euro for five.

After a short period of grace within her own camp, it was necessary to get back to reality and down to work in order to define the United Kingdom's position and formulate a strategy. The latter was announced by Theresa May in January 2017 in Lancaster

House – the same place where Margaret Thatcher announced British support for the single market in 1988 – in a speech given to an audience consisting of her Cabinet, European Union ambassadors, MPS and the press. The atmosphere was strange. Theresa May arrived, dressed in a green tartan trouser suit and looking a little tense. Then, as if someone behind the scenes had pushed her in order to nip her nervousness in the bud, she began to deliver her speech without any introduction whatsoever, not even the customary 'Ladies and gentlemen'.

The irony was that this speech, and with it the UK's whole Brexit policy, was delivered under a banner with the slogan *A Global Britain* as if to show by words – whereas actions tended to prove the contrary – that the United Kingdom was opening up to the world beyond the frontiers of Europe. I was sitting next to the German Ambassador and couldn't help whispering to him that Germany now knew what it had to do if it wanted at last to be able to trade with the rest of the world. As well as being hostile to foreigners, the speech was perceived as threatening, proclaiming that those countries wishing to punish Britain would be committing 'an act of calamitous self-harm' and that they would always need to sell their wines and cheeses and to buy British cars. But above all, Theresa May painted herself into a corner by adopting red lines that were untenable, while asserting – in order to please the most hard-line Brexiteers – that no deal was better than a bad deal. The break was to be total. The UK did not want to be half-in, half-out which meant leaving the single market, whereas several hard-line Brexiteers had said the contrary during the campaign. Lastly, she announced, on the basis of general principles only and without a real strategy, that Article 50 would be invoked in March 2017, thereby triggering withdrawal negotiations with the European Union and the two-year countdown towards the UK's projected departure date of 29th March 2019.

Civil servants had their roadmap. I went with my deputy, Jonathan, to visit the new Department for Exiting the EU shortly after it was set up. This department brought together, at Number

9 Downing Street, various officials from the European Affairs Department of the Foreign Office, the same department that had negotiated the reforms requested by David Cameron. The top specialists were not included – the British experts from the Commission who, in any case, would not have inspired confidence in London due to their European convictions, adopted a nationality that allowed them to continue working in the European institutions. The highly competent Permanent Representative of the United Kingdom to the European Union Ivan Rogers was pushed to resign for having dared to say, among other things, that Brexit would not be a single event occurring on a given date, but a process which would take years. I invited him to lunch at the Residence on his return to London. He felt he had done his duty as a civil servant to inform, warn and advise, in short to assist politicians in their decision-making. But the message was one they didn't want to hear, and so they shot the messenger.

Rogers' opinions were, nevertheless, shown to have been correct: three years after the vote, Brexit had still not taken place, first and foremost because its supporters themselves couldn't agree on how to define it. The date of final withdrawal had been fixed as 31 December 2020, after a year's transition period – *four and a half years* after the referendum. The problem was also that, from the beginning, the United Kingdom had refused to envisage, or even understand, a refusal by the club of the remaining 27 countries to redefine its founding rules in order to please the one that had decided to leave. Later, Ivan Rogers set out a summary of his opinions in a slim volume entitled 9 *Lessons in Brexit*.[2] Other EU experts – like the individual from the Treasury who knew the treaties and rules of the European Union by heart, or the head of the department in the Foreign Office responsible for the European Union – preferred to take a step back and work on other dossiers, sometimes as far away as possible in South America or Australia.

Ollie Robbins, the man who had been made responsible for the new Ministerial Department under the Secretary of State for Exiting the European Union David Davies, was intelligent and competent but had never had much to do with European affairs. The office that he had just moved into, and where he received us, was empty except for one thick, brand new volume: *The Treaty on European Union*. In the next-door office belonging to one of his colleagues, there was a single book on the table: *How to Negotiate*. Jonathan and I looked at each other, rather taken aback. They later had to recruit very expensive lawyers and experts in trade negotiations from Australia and New Zealand to make up for the lack of them in the UK since, for more than 40 years, responsibility for such matters had been devolved to the Directorate-General for Trade in Brussels. Extremely competent British officials had played their part there but it was impossible to recruit them there again, so some of them – committed Europeans who had spent their lives helping to construct Europe – applied for another nationality so as to be able to continue working in EU institutions.

David Davies and the Secretary of State for International Trade Liam Fox did nothing but say to anyone who would listen that everything would be fine. This same message was repeated over and over again to a delegation from the French National Assembly a few weeks after the referendum, without any detailed answers being given to the numerous questions posed. David Davies, who had confidently declared that it would be the easiest trade agreement to conclude in all human history, did not spend much time in Brussels and said one day that it was not necessary to be intelligent to be the minister for Brexit. Note duly taken.

Meanwhile, Theresa May continued mechanically to repeat the same meaningless mantra – 'Brexit means Brexit'. On returning from her annual Easter holiday walking in the Swiss mountains in April 2017, wishing to strengthen her hand and authority in negotiations with Brussels, she took everyone by surprise by calling a snap election. At which point a song by Captain SKA entitled 'Liar Liar' enjoyed great success on the airwaves and Twittersphere, given that she had said, on several occasions, that she would not call a general election.

It so happened that a few MPS – including John Brady, the chair of the famous 1922 Committee – had invited me to lunch in the dining room of Westminster on the very day of the last Prime Minister's Questions (PMQS) before the general election, and asked if I would like to attend. Guests sit in the balcony of this small, intimate chamber with green leather benches – known throughout the whole world thanks to films and television – and feel very close to the proceedings. On that day, Theresa May repeated at least 47 times, sometimes without any link to the question put by members of the Opposition, that the United Kingdom needed 'strong and stable government', which quickly became an ironic Twitter account under the name 'StrongerStabler'. In fact, all she needed to do was wave the Corbyn scarecrow in order to be cheered by the Conservatives. Sure of victory without the need for any real campaigning, she didn't think it necessary to take part in the last big televised debate and sent Amber Rudd instead, the minister who had succeeded her at the Home Office.

The gamble did not pay off. These elections proved once again that André Maurois was right when he said the outcome of elections in England was more difficult to predict than storms. Even though, in the preceding days, the press went to town with headlines such as 'Will June be the end of May?' all the polls gave reason to believe that her majority would be increased, so unpopular was Corbyn.

On 8th June 2017, I had been invited to dinner before watching the election results at the house of Roland Rudd – brother of the Home Secretary, founder and director of Finsbury Glover Hering, the public relations company – along with representatives or experts from all the political parties. Invited, in turn, to give their prediction as to the outcome, they were agreed in thinking that the result would give the Tories between 40 and 100 more seats. At 10pm: meltdown. Stupefaction when the result posted on the big screen showed that there was now a minority government, condemning Theresa May to form an alliance with the small, notoriously right-wing DUP Party from Northern

Ireland, thereby making herself their hostage. What astonished me most that evening was that, irrespective of party, everyone present – even the Conservatives – declared themselves satisfied with the result. Some even applauded. I remember Roland Rudd saying there was clearly not a majority in this Parliament for Brexit, a comment that was shown to be true in the months following. Before the election, young people from the world of theatre and cinema had told me they were going to use tactical voting to show their disapproval of Brexit – many others must have done the same.

Theresa May immediately fired her two unpopular advisers who were held responsible for this result. But they had also helped protect her, so now she completely lost authority over the members of her Cabinet: she began to be spoken of as an 'interim' prime minister. The former Chancellor of the Exchequer George Osborne, who was now editor-in-chief of the influential *Evening Standard*, held a grudge against her for not having offered him the job of foreign secretary. Appearing on the *Andrew Marr Show,* he unkindly described her as a 'dead woman walking' and said that the only question was how long she would remain on death row. She 'survived' for two years.

The Conservative Party Conference, which followed in October 2017, was a stark contrast to that of the previous autumn. Wearing a dark dress this time, Theresa May started by apologising, accepting responsibility for the disastrous general election result in June. To make matters worse, she was suffering from a bad cough which often obliged her to interrupt her speech; then a prankster tried to hand her a P45 form (given to an employee when they leave a job) on behalf of Boris Johnson; and the magnetised letters of the conference slogan – *Building a Country That Works For Everyone* – began to come unstuck, one by one, from the board that had been placed behind her. The fates were conspiring against her as, echoing the Americans, she talked about accomplishing the 'British dream', not something that Brexit is likely to inspire in young people. In comparison to the conference the preceding year which, in hindsight, showed the extent to which the Conservatives were living in a fantasy, the applause this time was more compassionate in nature and an encouragement to continue despite her bouts of coughing. What will be remembered from this speech of more than an hour is the series of misfortunes – it was generally considered to have been a fiasco.

Then Brexiteers began to turn against her and criticise her incompetence by failing to carry through the UK's withdrawal from the EU. Once again, she was said to be on the way out, but she showed herself to be remarkably resilient and lasted three years in total in spite of all the criticism and tribulations she suffered, falling between Scylla and Charybdis. She was not without humour, however, and after her inept attempts to dance with children on a visit to Africa had been roundly mocked on social media, she made her entrance at the next conference in 2018 by executing a few moves to Abba's 'Dancing Queen'.

After the excitement and illusions of her first months as prime minister and convinced that she had, at any cost, to succeed in carrying out this mission of Brexit with which she had been entrusted, Theresa May was able to take stock of the difficulties of the situation. Discussions with the 27 got properly under way after a 'phoney war' period, during which each side prepared its negotiation tactics with the greatest secrecy. Initially, she must have thought she could repeat the successful 'opt back in' exercise of 2016 (a cherry-picking approach of choosing, sector by sector, what the UK government wished to keep). For, as home secretary, she had opted out of some 130 regulations in the field of internal European affairs and justice, then negotiated hard to reintroduce only those provisions – 35 in total – that presented an interest for the United Kingdom, including the European arrest warrant. After a dinner in Downing Street in April 2017 with Jean-Claude Juncker, there were leaks to the German press about how he was flabbergasted to find out she was clearly living on another planet.

In the end, Theresa May showed herself to be more flexible in relation to her former red lines: a transition period of two years, payment of the sums due to the European budget, and a provisional solution to the Irish border question. I think that, while feeling obliged to assert that no deal was better than a bad deal, she sincerely wanted to reach a reasonable compromise agreement to ensure an orderly departure from the European Union.

In the summer of 2018, Theresa May decided to precipitate a trial of strength by organising a retreat with the members of her Cabinet at Chequers in order to thrash out a white paper on the United Kingdom's future relationship with the European Union. But, as I mentioned previously, it turned out to be a '*journée de dupes*' as Boris Johnson and David Davies resigned the following day, thereby adding to the confusion and the feeling that this saga would never end.[ii]

Theresa May personally took the negotiations in hand and travelled to Brussels herself on several occasions. (She also made a tour of the EU's main capital cities.) This resulted, without fuss, in a withdrawal agreement, a document of 579 pages adopted by the European Council in November 2018. Was this the end of the story? No, because the text had still to be ratified by the Parliament in Westminster and also by the European Parliament. Three unsuccessful attempts were made to get it through the House of Commons: it was rejected by a huge majority on 15 January, again on 12 March and finally on 29 March (which should have been the date of definitive withdrawal from the EU) in spite of an amendment in the margin of the accompanying political declaration, the chief EU negotiator Michel Barnier having made it clear that the text of the agreement itself could not be amended. On the basis of a rule dating back to Henry VIII, the Speaker of the House of Commons forbade a fourth attempt amidst sarcastic references to Einstein's definition of madness – doing the same thing over

---

[ii] 'Day of the Dupes', a reference to a day in November 1630 when the enemies of Cardinal Richelieu mistakenly believed that they had succeeded in persuading King Louis XIII of France to dismiss Richelieu from power.

and over again but expecting different results. I remember a seeing a cartoon that illustrated the impasse perfectly: Theresa May
dressed as an athlete with blood-stained bandages round her head
and knee about to try, for the umpteenth time, to jump over a bar
welded to a concrete wall, into which she inevitably crashed.

These successive failures are a perfect illustration of the contradictions of Brexit. The agreement was rejected not only by
the DUP and the most radical supporters of Brexit but also by
those wanting to retain a close link with the European Union. The
reality is that a good agreement was impossible since the British
already had the best deal they could have, as a member of the EU
that also enjoyed a large number of exemptions. Former prime
ministers John Major and Tony Blair, who always represented the
voice of reason, emphasised this fact. Some Brexiteers objected
to the text because it left the UK with less freedom and room for
manoeuvre than when it was a full member. The safeguard clause
(backstop) – required by the European Union to avoid the border
between the two Irelands becoming a target for smugglers, and by
Dublin to avoid a hard border reigniting conflict and endangering
the peace achieved thanks to the Good Friday Agreement – was
not the only problem. The backstop was very much resented
by the Brexiteers since it risked keeping Northern Ireland, and
the whole of the United Kingdom, in the single market until a
definitive agreement was concluded. Another fundamental truth
that the Brexiteers had difficulty in understanding was that, even
though the United Kingdom was an important country, it was to
other members of the union, in this case to the Republic of Ireland, that solidarity was due.

The fact that the United Kingdom had to ask for a first, then
later a second, postponement meant that it was obliged to vote
in the European elections in May 2019. This turned out to be a
humiliation for the Conservatives who came fifth with only four
seats, but a triumph for Nigel Farage whose newly formed 'Brexit
Party' took 31 per cent of the vote and 29 seats in the European Parliament, where its representatives played a provocative

role, turning their backs during the opening session at which the European anthem – Beethoven's 'Ode to Joy' – was played over loudspeakers. But the 16 Lib Dem MEPS, their party having come second with nearly 20 per cent of the vote, also made quite an entrance into the European Parliament by wearing their yellow T-shirts bearing the punchy slogan of their campaign, 'Bollocks to Brexit', thereby showing that there were British people who felt European and wished to stay in the EU.

Meanwhile, in London, Theresa May proposed negotiations with the Opposition in desperation, which came to nothing, and then allowed MPS to put forward their own suggestions. Eight options were identified by the Speaker of the House of Commons, but each of them failed to win a majority. 'No. No. No. No. No. No. No. No' was the front page of *The Guardian* on 28 March 2019.[3] Eventually, the time had arrived for Theresa May to be convened by the 1922 Committee, which had given her one last chance. She was told that she no longer enjoyed the confidence of the party and that she should resign which, with a heavy heart, she did on 24 May with effect as from 7 June 2019. Close to tears, she expressed her regret at not having been able to carry out her mission – 'Brexit means Brexit' – which she herself had described as 'sacred'.

A prisoner of the Northern Irish DUP and of the fanatical Europhobes of her own party who had formed the European Research Group (ERG) – chaired by Jacob Rees-Mogg, a caricature of a haughty old Etonian and Oxford graduate, nicknamed the 'honourable member of the 18th century',[iii] who became a laughing stock on social media – she had not had the time to accomplish anything else as prime minister. Brexit devoured her entirely, as

---

[iii] Jacob Rees-Mogg had demanded that the suffix 'Esq' – short for Esquire, from the old French 'escuyer' (shield-bearer) – be attributed to all men without a title. Larry the cat, the mouser in chief at Number 10 Downing Street, lost no time in adding 'Esq' to his name on his Twitter account....

it devoured the country, obsessed with this single issue for more than three years and all but absent from the international scene. Perhaps had she been more imaginative or creative she could have explained that a 'no deal' would be damaging to the country and that the withdrawal agreement negotiated in good faith was the only realistic one on offer. She could have suggested that it be submitted to the people for approval, failing which they would be given the choice of leaving without an agreement or staying in the European Union. This would have been the most democratic approach inasmuch as it would not have amounted simply to a second referendum, calling the first one into question. It was also no doubt the most opportune moment to do this. Indeed, by forming his new Brexit Party at this time, Nigel Farage was in reality girding his loins in preparation for a return to battle – whether referendum, general election or European elections. I sometimes wonder whether he is not one of those people who enjoys the journey more than the arrival at the destination. Other radical Brexiteers, on the other hand, aware that polls predicted a majority for Remain if there were to be a second referendum and realising that time was not on their side, began to panic. They became extremely aggressive, fearing that Brexit was about to slip through their grasp. The extreme right came out to demonstrate on the streets.

With their never-failing sense of humour, the British resuscitated the rallying cry used in 1940 – 'Keep Calm and Carry On' – which appeared on posters, mugs and T-shirts alongside a new slogan: 'Time to Panic!'

Three years later, a compromise was reached through negotiation but was not ratified by this Parliament in which the divisions quite simply reflected those in the country as a whole. It was, then, a fair fight and not – as has been claimed by Brexiteers of bad faith – a case of a parliamentary elite opposing the will of the people. Nor was it a case of people not knowing what they wanted, as was said in some European countries, comparing the situation to that of a cat that meows for someone to open the door but, once the door has been opened, no longer wants to go out. Those who opposed 'Theresa May's agreement', as it came to be called, came from two camps: on the one hand, extremists opposed to maintaining any link with the European Union and to the backstop; on the other, those who courageously, at the risk of being deselected or expelled, put the interests of their country above those of their party. The latter camp drew attention to the drawbacks of the compromise agreement for the United Kingdom and asked, at the least, for the people to be allowed to vote on it. First and foremost, the Father of the House Ken Clarke, the only Conservative to have voted from the outset against invoking Article 50 which triggered the divorce proceedings with the European Union, declared that he was putting the interests of his country above those of his party. The others, terrified of being accused of not respecting the outcome of the referendum and of betraying the supposed will of the people, only reacted once this agreement had been submitted.

Too late – the process had been started. They were subjected not only to criticism but also to insults and death threats, which obliged them to ask for police protection. Those concerned were the remarkable former Attorney General Dominic Grieve, an incisive debater, and Anna Soubry, who might be described in French as a *'grande gueule'*.[iv] To these should be added a number of centrists from the Labour Party, despite a leader who was clearly anti-European, and of course the SNP and lastly the Lib Dems, the only ones authentically pro-European to the point where – no doubt mistakenly, since they performed very badly at the elections – they said they were in favour of revoking Article 50.

The usual procedure for appointing a new Tory Party leader was launched by the 1922 Committee. There were six candidates so, after the organisation of televised debates, the process

---

[iv] Literally, a 'loudmouth' but can be used, as here, to describe someone who speaks forcefully and in a forthright manner.

of successively eliminating those with the fewest votes began. One of the candidates was Secretary of State for International Development Rory Stewart, so young-looking in both face and figure, a former diplomat and great walker who once took two years to walk across Afghanistan. He was the only one clearly against leaving without a deal and for a time enjoyed some support. At the end there were two candidates left in the contest but the die was cast and Boris Johnson won hands down against the moderate and courteous Foreign Secretary Jeremy Hunt, a former Remainer who, for political reasons, had to declare himself in favour of a 'no deal'. He ended up leaving politics, refusing to become a member of Boris Johnson's Cabinet.

Boris Johnson's longstanding ambition was about to be realised when – on 23 July 2019 – he entered through the door of Number 10 Downing Street with his new partner, Carrie Symonds, and his dog Dilyn. Advised by the Rasputin-like, emaciated and sardonic Dominic Cummings, the victorious strategist of the Leave campaign, and surrounded by Brexiteers of the most extreme variety (with the exception of Amber Rudd and his brother Jo, both of whom resigned a few weeks later) he chose to force Brexit through. This 'do or die' approach included trampling over Parliament – which he tried to muzzle for a period of five weeks – and lying to the Queen in the process, under the pretext, devoid of all credibility, that this was necessary in order to begin a new legislature whereas a period of one week would have been sufficient. In the country of *habeas corpus* and of *Magna Carta* – the 800th anniversary of which had been celebrated with great pomp four years earlier – that likes to think of itself as the first to introduce the rule of law and democracy, the Prime Minister did not hesitate to let it be understood that he would not comply with the law and that he would rather be 'dead in a ditch' than delay Brexit. The new date fixed for this momentous event was 31 October 2019, Halloween. He did not hesitate either to challenge the lower court's decision by appealing to the highest court in the land, the Supreme Court, which unanimously confirmed that his prorogation of Parliament had been illegal. It was, to say the least, astonishing to hear him say that this judgment was 'wrong', but Brexiteers lost no time in saying that the Supreme Court should be abolished. The most shocking session in the House of Commons was the one during which Boris Johnson described as 'humbug' the worry expressed by a female MP about the possible renewal of attacks similar to the one on Jo Cox, pointing out that Boris' use of inflammatory language such as 'traitors' and 'surrender' was encouraging those who were violently targeting female MPS in particular.

On 14 October, the day of the Queen's Speech – a general statement of policy written in its entirety by the prime minister and marking the opening of Parliament – the Queen, dignified as ever in spite of it all, read out the speech in a monotone, every sentence beginning with the traditional 'My Government' and including a statement that said the Government had always wished to leave the European Union on 31 October. On this occasion, the satirical weekly *Private Eye* republished its front page of some decades previously – a photo of Her Majesty reading out the Queen's speech with the caption 'and I hope you realise I didn't write this crap'.[4]

If, in the end, anyone did leave on 31 October it was the Speaker of the House of Commons John Bercow who had, with panache, acted the leading role in the play performed every night in the theatre of Westminster. He was forced out by Boris Johnson and the Brexiteers, who accused him of leading the rebellion against leaving the European Union. A photo on the cover of *Private Eye* which proved popular on social media consisted of an empty ditch with a caption saying 'Boris has let me down'.[5]

After a marathon round of discussions, Boris Johnson signed a withdrawal agreement with Jean-Claude Juncker on 17 October 2019. The Commission and the other 27 countries had had enough of this intractable dossier and really wanted to get on with other business. It was the second option that was retained as regards the main stumbling block: Ireland. This meant that, rather than a land border between the North and the South, there would be a maritime border between the United Kingdom and Northern Ireland, to be administered by the British authorities. Summoned to a 'super Saturday' – in reference to the last time the House of Commons had sat on a Saturday, dating back to the Falklands War – MPS were so distrustful of Boris Johnson that they demanded the adoption of implementing measures before they would vote on the text. At the same time, hundreds of thousands of people from all over the country (including the north-east of England where there had been a massive vote in favour of Brexit in 2016) congregated at Westminster, waving European flags and asking for a second referendum. Boris Johnson was obliged to postpone the date of leaving once again, this time for three months. But, manipulative as ever, he sent the President of the European Council contradictory letters in this regard. The first, unsigned, was a pretence of compliance with the law asking for a postponement while the second was signed by himself and sent together with another from his Permanent Representative saying that he did not want this postponement. The European Union decided to ignore these shenanigans and grant the request for a postponement.

All the initiatives taken by Boris Johnson, who seemed to be being pursued by the curse of Brexit, failed in the House of Commons. Undaunted, he may have lost these battles, but not the war. His ultimate goal was to hold a general election so as to obtain the public consecration that Theresa May never had, and hopefully to remain in power for the next ten years. This election in December 2019 was one that he was sure to win, given the extent to which Corbyn had become a bogeyman, even within his own party. And he did indeed win, hands down – he even conquered the 'red wall' of the North, Labour's traditional heartland. Here again, his populist demagogue tactics paid off. And the new slogan of his campaign chosen by Dominic Cummings – 'Get Brexit Done' – was powerful in its simplicity and brooked no argument.

A chapter of Brexit was brought to a close that day, after three and a half years of divisions, dogmatism, incoherence and above all, as seen from Brussels, indecision. Overnight, the subject that had dominated all political, economic and social debate for all that time more or less disappeared (even if the terms of the future relationship with the European Union still had to be negotiated). We have surely not heard the last of Brexit.

CHAPTER 7

Goodbye European Union;
Hello Post-COVID, Post-Brexit World

ON 31 JANUARY 2020, nearly four years after the referendum gave victory to Brexit (or 1,318 days and one hour, according to the exact tally kept by *The Times,* published the very next day[1]) the United Kingdom – after several postponements – formally left the European Union. Boris Johnson celebrated this memorable evening with his colleagues and Brexit supporters in Downing Street where English food only was served, washed down with an English sparkling wine. Beforehand, Boris Johnson had organised a symbolic Cabinet meeting in Sunderland, the city in the north-east, home to the Nissan factories, which had given the first indication that Leave was going to win. The Brexiteers, who had always feared a second referendum, which could have robbed them of their victory, were jubilant. As the fateful hour of 11pm approached, Brexit supporters flocked to Parliament Square bearing aloft the Union Jack as well as the English flag – the red cross of St George on a white background, normally only seen at sporting events. At the same time in Brussels, where it was midnight, the flag of the United Kingdom was lowered without ceremony.

This was the first time a member state had left. A sad moment; the end of 47 years of living together. Divorce had been pronounced but would not be finalised until the end of the transition period, scheduled for 31 December 2020. (This intervening period was to be used to reach agreement on the future relationship with the European Union.) Boris Johnson finally got what he wanted: the job of Prime Minister, and Brexit. His sole obsession now was to demonstrate the 'fantastic' results he'd been boasting about for four years.

In the middle of this euphoria (which coincided with the prospect of his becoming a father again), Boris Johnson – after spending Christmas on Mustique, the millionaires' island – took two weeks' holiday in February at Chevening, the country residence of the foreign secretary that he had once occupied. As far as he was concerned, there was nothing like the glorious kingdom of Her Majesty, the country of Brexit and the NHS. China was a far-off country with strange eating habits and a totalitarian system; it went without saying that the hospital service in Italy, being a southern European country, must be deficient, and France wasn't much better.

This cognitive bias – which also delayed measures to help combat the pandemic in other countries – in London took the form of British exceptionalism. It took a long time to understand that this 'black swan event', coronavirus, had arrived on the island and was going to cause considerable damage. Normally, it was the prime minister who chaired COBRA crisis meetings but, as the British people discovered later, Boris Johnson chose not to attend the first five such meetings devoted to the health emergency. Obsessed with Brexit, his first reaction was one of denial, adopting a cavalier attitude and encouraging the British to exercise their 'sacred right' to go to the pub, encouraged in this by his 79-year-old father, Stanley.

Notwithstanding the delays caused by the reluctance of the local authorities in Wuhan and Hubei to give bad news to the emperor, and Beijing's attempt to postpone notifying the WHO of the transmission from animal to man, on 11 January the Chinese published all the information at their disposal regarding the genome sequencing of the virus. On 11 March, the WHO declared the existence of a pandemic. Nevertheless, two days later, the annual Cheltenham horse racing festival, attended by more than 250,000 people, was allowed to go ahead which, without doubt, helped propagate the virus. It was not until 23 March that the

United Kingdom went into lockdown, after the idea of herd immunity had been abandoned.

Just weeks before, Boris Johnson boasted that he was continuing to shake everyone's hand, including in hospitals that were receiving COVID patients. And then on 27th March he announced in a video, in which he looked really ill, that he had contracted a benign form of COVID-19, before the information was broadcast the following Sunday that his doctors had decided to transfer him to an intensive care unit in hospital. There followed a period of a few days of uncertainty, during which the media wondered who was running the country.

The only anchor in all this was the Queen who pronounced a thoughtful speech of just less than four minutes, encouraging optimism. Obsessed with getting Brexit done, Boris Johnson hadn't appointed the best and the brightest to his Cabinet but rather the most ideologically 'pure'; this became very clear during his hospitalisation. The person he had appointed to replace him for urgent matters was the Foreign Secretary Dominic Raab, someone he was sure did not have the calibre to be prime minister. Once again, questions were raised about the need for a written constitution.

There was great relief when the person whom many considered to be a fighter returned to command the troops, even though people who had suffered serious illnesses, such as cancer, made the point on social media that in those circumstances, a human being is not a fighter but is, in fact, the battlefield. So, luckily, he recovered and thanked the medical staff – foreigners for the most part – who had helped him pull through. (He told *The Sun* that his doctors were, at one point, wondering how to break the news of his death to the nation, a scenario similar to Stalin's demise.[2]) Boris Johnson spent a few weeks recovering and then returned to Downing Street and Parliament, somewhat changed. Fatigue was a factor but, above all, he could no longer rely on his party trick of escaping from a difficult situation – with a pirouette – by making his audience laugh.

According to his biographer Andrew Gimson, this had been his favourite tactic ever since Eton.[3]

This became obvious at the weekly Prime Minister's Questions in the House of Commons, where he no longer had opposite him the unpopular Jeremy Corbyn. Instead, it was Kier Starmer: a Queen's Counsel, mild-mannered, certainly, but extremely rigorous and incisive, elected without fuss to the leadership of the Labour Party during the lockdown in April 2020. I met him when he was shadow Brexit secretary; he had an excellent reputation within the party, where he was thought to have a promising future. For the first time in five years, there was a capable Opposition in Parliament with a leader who was not, unlike his predecessor Jeremy Corbyn, unelectable. His popularity was growing, overtaking Boris Johnson's during the health crisis, and the prime minister's sputtered and vague replies suffered in comparison. For a while, Boris Johnson's brush with death won him some sympathy, but his management of the health crisis was judged to be amongst the worst in the world – along with that of Donald Trump and Jair Bolsonaro. The result was that the United Kingdom suffered one of the highest death tolls in Europe (over 70,000 at the end of the year 2020). A shortage of tests, masks, gloves, protective clothing and respirators; lies and little obfuscations, for instance counting gloves separately rather than in pairs.

Sympathy was replaced with anger, all the more so because many of those working in healthcare who died did so as a result of lack of adequate protection. This anger turned to fury when Boris Johnson's maleficent twin, Dominic Cummings – his special adviser with exorbitant powers, even over Cabinet ministers – broke the rules he himself had laid down. He left London while suffering from COVID in order to take his son to his parents in Durham, before taking his wife, also ill, to celebrate her birthday in a castle. His excuse was ridiculous: he had wanted to test if his eyesight was good enough to drive as far as London. The fury was so widespread, amongst the Tories also, that there were calls for him to resign. Jokes were legion, including a cartoon of

Boris Johnson saying he couldn't fire Dominic Cummings until Cummings instructed him to do so. This reflected the PM's degree of dependence on the gifted strategist who had first won Brexit for him, and then the election in December 2019. Boris Johnson knew that he owed his position as prime minister to Dominic Cummings. However, soon after the election of Joe Biden – and following a psychodrama – Darth Vader left Downing Street, thereby seeming to open the door to a less rigid position on Brexit.

The conditions Johnson set for coming out of lockdown were vague and actually refused by Scotland, Wales and Northern Ireland, as competence for matters of health had been devolved. Each of the four nations adopted its own policy as regards managing the crisis and Scotland's First Minister, Nicola Sturgeon, a woman of exceptional character, even declared her intention to close the border with England – a foretaste of the quarrels to come after the full restitution of the powers that were devolved to the European Union.

Meanwhile, time was running out for conclusion of Brexit negotiations. Even in 'normal' circumstances, this was an extremely tight deadline and, given lockdown, it seemed like mission impossible. To begin with, the two negotiators, Michel Barnier and David Frost, both tested positive for COVID; discussions continued via video conference but no progress was made. The British proved to be intransigent on all points and even backtracked on the political declaration that Boris Johnson had agreed to in October 2019 and which outlined the way forward. In September 2020, he provoked the European Union by presenting a bill to the Westminster Parliament on the internal market in breach of the agreement he himself had signed. He then tried to use the approaching deadline to force the hand of the Europeans at the last minute. His objective was more political than economic: as far as he was concerned, it was a question of affirming British sovereignty even though this was not the purpose of a free trade agreement that was designed to eliminate quotas and customs duties. This ideological dimension explains – though does not excuse – the threat he made a few days before the outcome of the negotiations, stalled on fishing rights, to dispatch Royal Navy ships to confront foreign fishing boats, mostly French ones.

It was a return to the longstanding illusion that the Europeans needed the United Kingdom more than the United Kingdom needed the Europeans. Boris Johnson only wanted to negotiate bilaterally with the UK's main partners, Emmanuel Macron and especially Angela Merkel (who was the president of the European Union during the second half of 2020). He considered that it was for heads of state and government to agree on the broad principles, leaving the 'nitty gritty' to be worked out by teams of negotiators. But the details are of fundamental importance – border controls, fishing rights, rules of competition, compliance with environmental and social norms, and so on. Boris Johnson, however, let it be known that he categorically refused to prolong the transition period for one or two years as had been suggested by the European Union. This was not unreasonable given that the United Kingdom, which had legally left the European Union, was still bound by European legislation that it had no influence over since it no longer took part in the decision-making process. Moreover, London had no intention of contributing to the substantial package of financial assistance the EU was planning to give to the countries most affected by the pandemic. The option of a hard Brexit, therefore, took centre stage once again. Both sides were weary, suffering from Brexit fatigue (another French word), and the United Kingdom, like the 27, had made their preparations accordingly.

The election of Joe Biden seemed to have changed things: now that he is in power, the moment for the necessary 'reconstruction' of international relations is approaching. In spite of the hopes of some countries, such as Germany, who have suffered more than others from the transatlantic fracture, this will not be a simple return to the *status quo ante*. Apart from anything else, the shift towards isolationism, the withdrawal from the affairs of the world, protectionism, and the priority given to the Pacific area rather than the continent of Europe – no longer seen as being as important – had already begun under President Barack Obama.

And what of the United Kingdom's obsession, when it was a member of the EU, with the risk of disruption to the transatlantic relationship? London will have little say in the matter and, when formulating diplomatic policy, will no doubt have to choose between purely adhering to the American position, or an alignment with the European Union given the shared concerns arising from geographical proximity.

At the very end of 2020, Brussels and London managed, with great difficulty, to agree on guidelines for their future relationship. But the work is far from being finished: the 1,246-page agreement, conveyed to London by the RAF, does not cover several important subjects (such as foreign policy, security and financial dealings). This is the first time that an agreement had to be negotiated to govern divergence from the European Union, rather than convergence with it. Given the time constraints, it amounts to a bare minimum agreement. This did not stop Boris Johnson from again pronouncing on high that the UK had – glory be – recovered its sovereignty. (As if France, Germany and Italy were not sovereign nations.) The limitation of European fishing rights was considered important essentially for its symbolic character – the sector represents only 0.01 per cent of Britain's GDP, whereas the City, which represents seven per cent, was not included. Services, which account for 80 per cent of the UK's exports, were not included either. And participation in the Erasmus programme, very popular with young people, was abandoned. Once the bitterness of the divorce has dissipated on both sides, it will be in the interests of London and of the European capitals to construct a partnership that is both multidimensional and mutually beneficial.

On 31 December 2020 at midnight, continental time, 11pm Greenwich Mean Time, as the long-silent Big Ben struck, the United Kingdom cut all its institutional ties with the European Union. A return to 'splendid' isolation which, it may be remembered, ended in 1904 with the *entente cordiale*.

In any event, the UK is starting a new chapter in its history and will have to do so while facing the double challenge of Brexit and COVID which has already given rise to the new word, 'Brovid'. The economic consequences of the pandemic have already been disastrous, with an unprecedented drop in GDP of 20.4 per cent for April 2020, the first month of lockdown. The OECD forecast that the UK will be the country hardest hit. The result will be a recession of historic proportions.

The temptation will be to continue to sweep the bill for Brexit under the COVID carpet and to hide behind the worldwide economic crisis. (This bill was estimated by Bloomberg to amount to over £200 billion for 2020, nearly as much as the UK's total contributions to the European Union since joining in 1973: £215 billion.) Strangely, many ordinary people, as well as Brexit fanatics, said during the campaign that they wouldn't mind being poorer if they were independent. Mission accomplished. Interestingly, even if it no longer matters from a practical point of view, pro-European sentiment has grown in the United Kingdom, a poll in the autumn of 2020 giving a clear majority of 60 per cent in favour of the EU.

For over four years, the British have been talking amongst themselves. Now they will have to speak to the world, and not just speak but enter into dialogue and, most importantly, negotiate. The idea that, once free of its European shackles, the United Kingdom can at last reach out to the whole world under the banner of 'Global Britain' – which, by the way, nothing was preventing it from doing while remaining in the EU – may well prove to be illusory.

The UK's attempts, so far unsuccessful, to negotiate an agreement with Australia – a country it has close ties with but, even together with New Zealand, accounts for only 0.01 per cent of its foreign trade compared to 47 per cent for the European Union – is a good illustration of this twisted vision of reality. Even India, where relations are sensitive given the shared colonial past accounts for only an infinitesimal share of the UK's foreign trade.

The United Kingdom does more business with the Republic of Ireland than it does with China; negotiations with Canberra and New Delhi stalled on the question of visas – student ones in particular – which London refused to grant, since limiting immigration was one of the key arguments for Brexit. Having said that, the UK, in the face of increased Chinese pressure on Hong Kong and the adoption of the national security law, decided to grant 3 million Hong Kong citizens the right to stay in the United Kingdom for five years, and then acquire British nationality, despite having been very parsimonious in this regard at the time of the handover in 1997. A free trade agreement with Japan has been signed with great pomp and ceremony, but it is a simple cut and paste exercise based on the agreement Tokyo had with the European Union. This is true also of the agreements London hurried to sign with other countries, so as not to lose the advantages the EU had already negotiated. *Tout ça pour ça?* Was it really worth all that for such a result?

The fact remains that the post-Brexit United Kingdom will have to reorganise its relations with the rest of the world and in particular with the United States and China, whose rivalry will be the dominant feature of the coming decades. How can this be achieved when going it alone? What are the possible alliances or partnerships? What are the risks of being marginalised, exploited or blackmailed? The members of the Commonwealth have never shared London's illusions and have always expressed their incredulity at the decision to leave the EU. A recent cartoon in *The New Zealand Herald* depicted an Englishman delighted to be leaving the European Union in order to meet up with his new 'chums', while at the next corner a panda and Uncle Sam were lying in wait, each armed with a large club.[4]

The corollary for the European Union of this weaker UK no longer enjoying the influence of membership of the world's largest trading block, is a loss in economic terms (the UK being the world's fifth largest economy) and also in terms of international outreach. But this loss can be offset by the fact that there will no longer be a British brake on progress in matters of defence and economic integration. Thus, the historic decision agreed to by the Germans on 18 May 2020 – authorising, for the first time, joint borrowing on the market of €750 billion in order to assist those countries hardest hit by the economic consequences of the COVID crisis – strengthens the foundations of Europe. The lifting of this taboo consolidates the European Union, suffering as it was due to the pandemic.

This ambitious stimulus plan was an incentive for London to leave the EU at the end of 2020, for fear of having to pay part of the cost. But even though it is in the interests of the United Kingdom to have its principal partner enjoy economic prosperity, strong European recovery supported by Germany sends a signal that is not to the UK's advantage: it is easier to sell Brexit if things are going badly on the continent. The UK's third application for EU membership, which came to fruition in 1973, was made at a time when the economy of the European Union was thriving while the United Kingdom's was in the doldrums. This recovery plan and new European project together put France at the heart of the action and reactivated the Franco-German engine which had long lain dormant. This is all the more significant as the dialogue with Germany did not get off to a good start after Brexit. It is true that the triangular relationship often helped encourage Germany to agree on Franco-British initiatives, and conversely. A joint position agreed by the three capitals was of benefit to the EU but London and Berlin, more liberal, could also agree between themselves on issues, which could put France in a difficult position.

The COVID pandemic did not change the world overnight, but it did reveal and highlight certain realities and underlying trends. These presented challenges for the members of the European Union as well as for the United Kingdom since they risked being marginalised by two giants, which are today engaged in an all-out cold war.

* * *

The excessive hopes about a democratisation of China expressed just before Xi Jinping took up office were certainly due to the fact that his father was a genuine moderate at a time when it was particularly dangerous and brave to be so. Xi Jinping is a nationalist and, echoing Donald Trump, wants to 'make China great again' by fulfilling the Chinese dream to be a great and respected power by the centenary in 2049 of the founding of the People's Republic of China. Before that, 2021 marked the centenary of the creation of the Chinese Communist Party and the declared goal of making China a 'moderately prosperous society'. For Xi Jinping, the future of China is the same thing as the future of the Communist Party, which explains in part his decision to remain in power without any limit as to time. Perhaps also because of ambition, a taste for absolute power, a desire to protect himself against all the enemies he made during his all-out campaign against corruption, so as to be able to carry through his ambitious programme without becoming a 'lame duck' like his Western counterparts during election campaigning. His 'best friend' Vladimir Vladimirovitch Putin learned the lesson by amending the Russian Constitution in the summer of 2020 to allow him to remain in power, in theory, for two additional mandates of six years each.

Contrary to what may be said or read, China is not in the least interested in the regimes of the states it does business with. Its approach is pragmatic and the saying made famous by Deng Xiaoping: 'it doesn't matter if the cat is black or white as long as it catches mice', remains valid in all circumstances. Beijing doesn't care if a country is a dictatorship, a democracy, a failed state or corrupt, as long as it isn't bankrupt (and not even then, since this can facilitate the purchase of infrastructures). Its policies and diplomacy are guided by the logic of power and have no moralising or evangelical side to them. If the 'Beijing Consensus' – a term invented by the Americans – appeals to African nations, it is because of the proven success of its economic policies and because China's interest in Africa, in particular through the building of infrastructure, has enabled the continent, abandoned by the West, to open up and continue to develop. African ambassadors to Beijing are very clear on this point in spite of the criticisms that have been levelled at the methods used by the Chinese – which have actually evolved over the years – and the racism that was evident in Canton during the coronavirus pandemic.

What China no longer tolerates, since rising to become the second-ranking world power, is being lectured to, especially by governments or regimes that it judges to be less successful economically and in crisis politically. It is true that China overplayed its hand when trying to present itself as an efficient and generous power through the use of 'mask diplomacy', but it did work up to a point, notably in Africa and at first in Italy which once again suffered from a lack of solidarity from its European partners. In Italy, at the end of the first wave of SARS-COV-2, China was more popular than Germany, something which Angela Merkel alluded to in a long interview she gave to European newspapers in June 2020. However, the inappropriate comments made by the young and ultra-nationalistic 'wolf warrior' diplomats, criticising democratic regimes on the social media of their embassies in the countries they were accredited to, were obviously not well received and gave rise to unprecedented hostility towards China. But the aim of such heavy-handed propaganda – tactless and counter-productive – was no doubt less to convert the West as to demonstrate to the Chinese people that democracies are weak and less efficient in dealing with a health crisis than an authoritarian regime.

Beijing is not so naive as to think it can persuade London, Paris, Berlin or Washington to adopt its political system but Chinese propaganda, like the Russian variety, doesn't miss an opportunity to report on – and sometimes exaggerate – any popular demonstration in our countries complete with accusations of police or racial violence, thus relativising their own radical methods of controlling the Chinese population, in particular the Uighurs. The Chinese press went to town on reporting the post-electoral chaos in the USA, when Donald Trump refused to concede to Joe Biden.

This was another reason to criticise democracy, which served the interests of internal Chinese propaganda well by demonstrating the comparative wisdom of their leader and stability of their regime. In 2013, in an attempt to increase openness, the powerful Propaganda Department of the party was renamed the 'Information Department' in English but without changing the name in Chinese. The approach remains rather Soviet in nature.

Having seen the hostility generated by the arrogant and belligerent attitude adopted by the 'wolf warriors', the Chinese authorities did, however, change tactics and stopped using their embassies to criticise European governments. And their policy of supplying developing countries with low-cost vaccines has been conducted more discreetly than their mask diplomacy.

China was the first country to return to growth (over 1.9 per cent) in 2020, to increase exports significantly and to increase its share of world trade, reprising its role as the locomotive of the world economy. Once again, the recurring doom-laden predictions were proved wrong. I remember, in 2008, the apocalyptic reports of Shenzhen workers being sent home *en masse*. For the umpteenth time, the Western press predicted the end of Chinese growth. In fact, it rebounded very quickly thanks to a recovery plan financed to the tune of 4,000 billion yuan; the essential infrastructure has largely been built since. But another growth model has already been adopted, one based on internal consumption and services and no longer simply on exports and investments.

There is no doubt that, in spite of its difficulties (regional indebtedness, social inequalities, ageing population), China has the energy and determination to bounce back. Xi Jinping is well aware that the credibility and popularity of the Communist Party, which today has 90 million members, are linked to the formidable economic success that has made it possible to extricate 800 million people from poverty and, in record time, raise China to the rank of second world superpower. The party has strengthened its grip by imposing cells in every enterprise. This may not be an ideal form of management but it hasn't affected growth or dampened the entrepreneurial spirit. As for Xi Jinping's popularity, it is true that he was criticised at the beginning of the epidemic in Wuhan, but the journal published by the writer Fang Fang – whose novels all describe with affection the ordinary people of her city – shows that, as in the days of the empire, criticism is aimed at the local mandarins rather than at the Emperor himself.[5] Generally speaking, although the intelligentsia's hopes of openness and liberalisation have been disappointed, the people appreciate the efforts made by Xi to combat corruption and protect growth and employment.

China, which for decades remained modest and discreet in accordance with the recommendations of Deng Xiaoping to bide its time while hiding its talents, is now proud of its success to the point of risking hubris, which is always dangerous. The size of its reserves and profits has encouraged China to launch other, more multilateral, initiatives such as the Asian Infrastructure Investment Bank (AIIB), and then the new silk roads strategy known as the 'Belt and Road Initiative' (formerly 'One Belt One Road') with the goal of strengthening China's trade links. Is the aim here to go beyond economic and commercial relations in order to achieve dominance? It is, in any event, a matter of prestige and of personal importance to Xi Jinping, who asserts that it also benefits the rest of the world. Above all, it is a means of ensuring a supply of raw materials, of selling excess production, for instance steel – which has affected the United Kingdom in particular – and opening up new markets. Investment in strategic sectors in Europe is now subject to stricter control; the United Kingdom, which can no longer serve as the gateway into Europe, is also reviewing its policy. The question of reciprocity has been raised by some of the more sceptical EU countries, but nothing obliges the return journey to be empty of freight. The question will not arise if we have produce to export, as exemplified by Germany which has retained a trade surplus with China. The principle of reciprocity should be applied instead to the opening up of procurement contracts. This ambitious Chinese project, involving 143 countries throughout the world, has led to divisions within the European Union, as Rome and Lisbon decided to sign up to it. It will be interesting to see the stance taken by the countries of Eastern Europe that, until the COVID crisis, have been the most 'pro-American' whilst at the same time enjoying a privileged relationship with China. It is essential for the European Union to adopt a strategy that is both firm and realistic. At an economic level, Europe has all the instruments it needs: encouraged by Angela Merkel and after seven years of negotiations, Brussels finally concluded an agreement on investments that greatly improves European access to the Chinese market while addressing European concerns about forced labour. The second victory won by Beijing is the signing of the free trade agreement, mentioned earlier, with countries of the region, including those it has had difficult relations with, such as Australia and Japan.

The other aspect of Chinese power that concerns the West is what is called 'entryism' in international institutions. But the Chinese feel – justifiably – that Western countries allocated all the influential positions to themselves, leaving them only the post of assistant secretary-general in the UN Department of Economic and Social Affairs (since they had to be given something). As always, China took a step-by-step approach. After the appointment of Margaret Chan, a Hong Kong graduate of American and Canadian universities, as director-general of the WHO, the next post targeted was the head of UNIDO (the United Nations Industrial Development Organization) which, by pure coincidence, France left the same year that the Chinese took charge. The next targets were the International Civil Aviation Organization (ICAO), the International Telecommunication Union (ITU), the Food and Agriculture Organization (FAO), Interpol and then the World Intellectual Property Organization (WIPO). China succeeded in achieving these goals, thanks in particular to African support. Can this be said to be illegitimate given that China is now the second-ranked world power and the second-largest contributor to the regular UN budget, that it has made available a reserve of 8,000 men for peacekeeping operations and that it is the permanent member that provides the most troops? It was indeed asked to do these things and was thanked accordingly by the Secretary-General of the UN. We ourselves kept asking China to increase its contribution and take on more responsibilities and now it has – though no doubt well beyond what we intended and not always in our interests.

There is now an imbalance in the system as China heads four specialised agencies out of 15 and often in sensitive areas where it is in a position to promote its own policies and interests. It is the only country to be over-represented at the head of UN agencies. It cannot be denied that China has expertise in agricultural matters but its record on standards in the field of justice and the police is questionable. Indeed, that particular appointment did not end well since the elected President of Interpol Meng Hongwei was, without ceremony, recalled to Beijing, accused of corruption. The same doubt could be expressed in relation to the World Intellectual Property Organization (WIPO) which is responsible for industrial intelligence and patents. It is true that China is the country that files the most patent applications in the world, but it still has some way to go in the field of intellectual property protection.

This situation is the result of American disengagement. Generally speaking, when campaigning for an appointment as head of an international agency, it is important for a country to choose its candidates on the basis of their expertise and experience, not because there is no longer a place for them at national level. I was witness to this when working as the director-general for the UN and international organisations at the Quai d'Orsay. Next, the campaign has to be well argued and conducted with the support of our partners – this approach made it possible to secure the election of Daren Tang, from Singapore, to be head of WIPO in May 2020, in preference to his Chinese competitor. What many people discovered with the COVID crisis and the 'case study' of the WHO, is that agencies can be influenced by their biggest donors, public or private. For instance, the Bill and Melinda Gates Foundation, the next biggest donor after the United States, was found to be targeting the eradication of poliomyelitis which was no longer a priority in the world. But the agencies are now financed to the tune of 80 per cent by voluntary contributions that are often earmarked for a particular purpose, with only 20 per cent coming from mandatory contributions. The former Ethiopian Minister of Health and Foreign Affairs Dr Tedros Adhanom Ghebreyesus was not the official candidate of China but of Africa, on the basis of the principle, not always applied, of geographical rotation. But he was known to have links with China and it is true that China enjoys particular influence in Ethiopia having invested heavily in that country, thereby boosting its economy. If we want to influence the governance of these agencies, we must stop continually reducing our voluntary contributions in an effort to save money. For, considering the subjects addressed, these technical agencies represent a good return on investment.

* * *

Multilateralism serves the interests of the Europeans – it's often said indeed that it's in their DNA. The Americans, on the other hand, think they can do without it. We must at least stop thinking – even subconsciously – that the European–American partnership should be dominating everything. Kishore Mahbubani, a brilliant diplomat and political analyst from Singapore, poses the (rhetorical) question in two recent well-argued books with provocative titles: *Has the West lost?*[6] and *Has China won?*[7] For his part, former French Minister of Foreign Affairs Hubert Védrine points to the fact that the West has lost the monopoly of power. There is, however, a new awareness, as shown by the choice of topic for the Munich conference just before the pandemic hit. The question of 'values' is a complex one and we would do better to choose 'rights' as the battleground, these being universal if only because of the 1948 Universal Declaration of Human Rights. The Chinese member of the drafting committee, Chang Pengchun, made a decisive contribution by persuading the other members of the committee to adopt the humanist principles of Confucianism and to resort to compromise. The other member who played an important role was the Lebanese Charles Habib Malik. But who remembers them, or wants to remember them, even in their own countries? René Cassin and Eleanor Roosevelt are the only names we have retained. It is clear that torture is not a 'value' in any culture.

We Westerners, on the other hand have, rightly or wrongly, been criticised by all the countries of the Far East, irrespective of their regime, for being individualistic and egotistical – perceived as Western traits – as opposed to Asian or Confucian values of attachment to community. Is democracy a universal right? And which system of democracy, since they are all different? Winning the most votes does not necessarily mean winning the election – as seen in the United States – and of course a sitting president may contest the results of an election, as happens in many African countries in particular (something for which they are lectured on by the Americans). A structure that is formally democratic does not always guarantee the rights of minorities or, for example, protect against discrimination on the basis of extremely rigid caste systems which tolerate ethnic violence.

With the arrival of new generations who have a better understanding of the world (in which they have studied and travelled) than the present generation of leaders formed by the communist system, China will evolve. Many, educated in the British system, remain profoundly nationalistic. In the meantime, we must stop dreaming that democratisation will automatically follow on economic growth and the emergence of a middle class. While we must still be ready to draw attention to flagrant breaches of human rights, it will be to our advantage to deal with countries and regimes as we find them. We should not be lecturing others, conveniently forgetting about our own failures and shortcomings, especially when even some EU countries do not apply the rule of law or respect democratic principles. We must prepare ourselves to live in a world where democracies exist alongside strong, illiberal regimes – we did so in the time of the Soviet Union. We found the criminal, Maoist version of China – far away and so culturally different, it is true – more attractive than a China that has become powerful and competitive, thanks to the vision of its leaders and the hard work of its people.

Events in this century will be determined by the increasing power of China and its rivalry with the United States. Europe will have to become a balancing power, continue to be a normative one and, most importantly, achieve veritable independence as regards defence, the economy and technology, ideally by setting up an American-style DARPA for research and development in relation to new military technologies.[i] It is vital to strengthen the euro and make it a real reserve currency. EU countries will have to agree on a realistic relationship with Beijing and Washington based on the interests of the Europeans, rather than automatically supporting, in Pavlovian fashion, the White House in its power struggle with China.

During his mandate Donald Trump, with his revisionist approach, destabilised Europe and the world more than Xi Jinping. Unilateralism is not new in American history, but the systematic demolition of the multilateral structure set up by America itself after the war, was indeed previously unseen. To the point where it cut its contributions to, and withdrew from, the World Health Organization in the middle of a pandemic, thereby offering Xi Jinping – who promptly announced an additional contribution of two billion dollars – the opportunity, once again, to take centre stage. From the beginning, Trump made clear that for him, it would be 'America first', and he implemented his programme to the letter without allies or friends but designating new enemies: first and foremost China, but also the Europeans

---

[i] DARPA: Defence Advanced Research Projects Agency.

with a special mention for Germany but with the exception, for reasons of ideological kinship, of the Brexitland of Nigel Farage and Boris Johnson. From the outset, he accused the Europeans of being enemies who took advantage of the United States by not paying NATO their share of the cost of their defence and who sold their – German – cars without importing American ones in return. After concluding the first phase of his trade agreement with China in January 2020, he declared in the clearest of terms that it was the turn of the Europeans next. On the first point, the French Defence Minister Florence Parly, retorted with cutting humour that Article 5 of the NATO Treaty, under which an armed attack against one member state automatically triggers a reaction from the others, was not Article F35, the name of the fighter aircraft which America was trying to impose on the alliance. In sum, the Europeans were to increase their defence budgets in order to buy American weapons. NATO had already been used, before Trump, to further Washington's interests and it will no doubt survive. Trump's initial reaction, in fact, had been to declare NATO obsolete in spite of the advice of his generals and the protestations of his allies.

The 45th President of the United States decided to withdraw American troops from certain combat zones – this was, perhaps, justified but to do it so suddenly and without consulting his allies in the theatres of war in the Middle East meant that Russia became master of the situation. Along with Ankara and Teheran, Russia was directing the Syrian crisis and was intervening in similar fashion with Turkey in Libya. Trump denounced the treaties signed by his predecessor, from the Paris agreement on climate change to the Iran nuclear deal; amongst other damage caused, this behaviour undermined the image of democracy, which suffered as a result. It had already been discredited by the election to the presidency of such an ignorant, lying and narcissistic buffoon spouting racism and xenophobia. The Chinese press wrote at the time of the 2016 electoral campaign, 'Democracy is a farce – look at Trump'. His capricious behaviour and catastrophic handling of the health crisis only confirmed this assessment – all the peoples of the world have at one time or another been flabbergasted or outraged by his aggressive or grotesque utterances, the high point being his ridiculous musings about possibly injecting bleach into people's lungs in order to clean them of COVID.

At the beginning of the COVID crisis, a poll conducted by the Pew Research Center showed that the degree of satisfaction of the Chinese with their leaders was amongst the highest in the world. Of course some in China or in Russia may not much like their leaders but they might not be ashamed of them,[ii] whereas many Americans expressed this sentiment during Trump's mandate. This was the person who separated young children from their parents and put them in cages, who encouraged people to revolt against the reasonable measures to combat COVID taken by states governed by Democrats, or who was hell-bent on supporting the Second Amendment on the carrying of arms by any criminal or mentally disturbed person at the cost of tens of thousands of deaths every year – many of them children. Such a person was certainly not best placed to give lectures on human rights. Indeed, the topic did not interest Trump in the slightest and his support for said rights was intermittent at best. The messenger killed the message. His fascination, tinged with affection, for the leader he called 'Rocket Man' – Kim Jong-un – must have puzzled the Chinese. They endeavoured to maintain the status quo in North Korea for reasons of self-interest, but they have no illusions about the man or the regime, reminiscent to them of the cultural revolution.

The hackneyed expression 'leader of the free world' made the situation worse since it included us all by association. Then, by making hostile declarations about multilateralism and free trade, Trump allowed Xi Jinping – since his noteworthy intervention at the Davos Forum of 2017 – to play the leading role

---

[ii] At least until the invasion of Ukraine. Even after this, it is still a relatively small minority of Russians that seem to be ashamed of their leader.

in championing these noble causes, albeit dressed in Chinese colours. Furthermore, while it is true that Western access to Chinese procurement contracts is limited, are American markets any more open? At least the Chinese don't impose their decisions by prohibiting the Europeans from dealing with specific countries, as do the Americans on the basis of extraterritorial laws, taking advantage of the supremacy of the dollar.

One of the consequences of Trump's policy was also – in line with the well-known principle that 'the enemy of my enemy is my friend' – to have encouraged a new honeymoon between Beijing and Moscow, despite the fact that these are two peoples who have had a chequered history and between whom there is no love lost. Although differing in style, the two leaders established a personal relationship that was consolidated further with each visit. On the Security Council, their positions are coordinated and no resolutions have been adopted on Syria since we effected 'regime change' in Libya, by eliminating Gaddafi and upsetting the two capitals as a result. They are now taking their revenge.

Putin also wanted to 'make Russia great again' by restoring its prestige and making it once more an important actor on the international stage, or at least in the Middle East and Africa. The relationship between the two countries is asymmetrical but Xi Jinping pretends not to notice this. There has been a spectacular reversal of their importance and influence over the last 30 years and China is now a geoeconomic power with a population of 1.4 billion, one fifth of the world's total, whereas Russia – with a GDP the same as that of Spain and a population (146 million) that is decreasing – retains a purely geopolitical vision of power where the size of the military is more important than that of the economy (a vision of the world inherited from the Soviet Union and the Cold War). An illustration of this was the speech given by Putin in March 2018 in the hall of the Moscow Manege when, against an impressive background picturing a hypersonic missile, a fireball, striking Florida, he uttered the following, very revealing sentence: 'Nobody listened to us, you will listen now'.

This was, according to his aides, an invitation to start a dialogue. He showed off these sophisticated weapons, which the Americans don't yet have, in order to try to restore a form of parity in what was the key sector of co-operation between Washington and Moscow at the time of the Cold War, co-operation in relation to which the Russians feel a certain nostalgia. The purchasing power of the population keeps on falling in a country excessively dependent on exports of gas and oil controlled by huge companies such as Gazprom and Rosneft. And that, despite the considerable reserves which were constituted as soon as the cost per barrel rose above $40, something which allowed Putin to offer himself the luxury of a dispute with Saudi Arabia by refusing to limit production so as to push the price up in February 2020. He did this in order to weaken the American producers of shale gas, in competition with Russian gas.

Trump's relationship with Putin was more complex than that with Xi Jinping. Trump was certainly fascinated by the latter, the strong man at the head of an empire, but he didn't really understand him. He also knew that China was the more dangerous competitor. With Putin, whom he understood better, he would have had more room for manoeuvre had his presidency not been tarnished by the suspicion of Russian interference in his election. That was the main reason why the Helsinki summit in 2018 proved a failure. During the joint press conference, Trump called into question the reliability of his own intelligence services and this gave rise to such an outcry in the US that relations afterwards with Russia were paralysed. But Russia is not likely to totally break the partnership – not an alliance – that it has established with China, which has become increasingly close in recent years, including at a strategic level with joint military exercises not only in the Far East but also in the Baltic.

Despite the assertions made by some, no particular regime has emerged the winner as such, neither East nor West, North nor South. Was this due to the happenstance of situations in different parts of the world? Reasons that we don't yet understand? Good or bad management? It is no doubt too soon to say. But the countries of the European Union – such as Belgium, Italy, Spain and France, have paid a heavy price, while Germany, Greece and the countries of Eastern Europe were initially relatively spared – must work together to rebuild solidarity and ensure recovery. The United Kingdom, which suffered even more than the continent, will have to manage the consequences of the pandemic at the same time as those of Brexit. It will have to redefine its relationship with its neighbours in order to steer the best course possible between Washington and Beijing.

In this Cold War context, the European Union must learn to understand the workings of power and arm itself with a strategic compass if it is to remain a player worthy of the name. It is interesting to note here that the United Kingdom opted to adhere to the (military) European Intervention Initiative, even though it had already started the process of withdrawing from the European Union. It is theoretically possible for the United Kingdom to join in with the EU's security and defence operations, but details as to the how and the why will have to be worked out. The joint positions of the three major capitals – Berlin, London, Paris – on subjects of mutual interest will also have to be agreed. An example here is Iran: an initiative dating back to 2003 aimed at bringing together the three capitals who were divided on the question of support for the American war in Iraq, but without alienating the other European capitals at the same time – a touchy subject – and weakening the European Union as such. The EU succeeded in asserting itself thanks to the tactics of the chief negotiator, Michel Barnier, who unfailingly played the transparency card with member states, thereby ensuring that solidarity was maintained.

Brexit came into force on 1 January 2021 but that is not the end of the story – modalities of co-operation, over and above the agreed texts, will have to be established.

Afterword

I SPENT OVER 40 years of my diplomatic career working in close collaboration, and more than that, close friendship and complicity, with my British colleagues, first as a young diplomat and then as an ambassador. In Beijing and Moscow, in *quad* or *quint*,[i] in the soundproof rooms of embassies, and in multilateral settings such as the United Nations in New York or in the EU's Political and Security Committee (COPS/PSC) in Brussels. I began my career at the very end of the '70s in the last jewel in the British Crown, the territory of Hong Kong.

I loved living in London, a dynamic city both modern and traditional, a 'city in the country' with its immense and magnificent parks, foxes and squirrels in the streets. I loved the lively intelligence of the renowned British sense of humour with its dose of self-deprecation. I loved the rigour of the professors in the great universities, the scientists, the lawyers and the journalists from media with a worldwide audience. I appreciated the countless debates in the think tanks. I had the privilege of meeting extremely talented, contemporary writers for whom an individual story is set in a particular context, a moment in history – Julian Barnes, William Boyd, Jonathan Coe, Kazuo Ishiguro, Ian McEwan, John le Carré, David Lodge. I also traced the lives of bygone authors in the countryside or small English towns – Bath for Jane Austen, Devon for Agatha Christie and Conan Doyle, and Cornwall for Daphné du Maurier. I wore a William Shakespeare mask at the procession organised in Stratford-upon-Avon to celebrate the 400th anniversary of his death.

---

[i] The former referring to France, Germany, the United Kingdom and The United States; the latter referring to France, Germany, Japan, The United Kingdom and the United States.

In short, I would happily have stayed, like my distant and illustrious predecessors – till he was over 80 in the case of Talleyrand, or for 22 years like Jules Cambon. I know that the life of an ambassador in London, between Kensington Palace Gardens and Knightsbridge, is an extremely privileged one, and that many of my young colleagues from the Foreign Office had to live at more than an hour's commute from London. The favour can be returned when they come to Paris.

I lived the Brexit years with intense interest – as French Ambassador I had a front-row seat and privileged access – but also with astonishment and sadness. For three years, I had met hundreds of people from all walks of life, sometimes very early in the morning over a working breakfast – a British tradition – at lunch, or dinner. In this parliamentary democracy, in addition to ministers, I met backbenchers – so influential – and members of the House of Lords. Although unelected, this chamber contains a wealth of experience and intelligence but is, nevertheless, constantly criticised, calls being made regularly for it to be put to death. Like the royal family and bishops – these latter being *ex officio* members of the House of Lords – they do not have the right to vote in general elections. I also often received journalists: invaluable sources of information, analysis and gossip. The French Residence was elegant and the food served there had an excellent reputation, in line with the advice of Talleyrand who said that 'a good chef is more important than a good embassy secretary' – no offence intended, needless to say, to my excellent team at the Chancery.

I often liked to meet with people individually, 'in confessional', so that they could give their opinions freely. And some also turned to me with their questions, believing that I was better informed than they were since I spoke to everyone, including their adversaries. With very rare exceptions, they all – Remainers and Leavers alike – were convinced, right up to the last minute, that the United Kingdom would refuse this leap into the unknown and would stay in the European Union.

It was difficult to grasp that things were changing and that bubbling under the surface, everywhere in the world, was hostility to the political, economic and financial elite. Globalisation was being challenged and new demands were being made based on identity. All this was served and amplified by social media, where hate and conspiracy theories based on 'alternative facts' were the order of the day, while the term 'fake news' was adopted everywhere (we finally invented an equivalent term in French: *infox*). Even experts no longer found favour in the eyes of the people, as in the time of the Chinese cultural revolution (the acme of populism) when it was said that it was better to have a socialist train that arrived late, than a capitalist one that arrived on time, that it was better to be red (a Brexiteer) than an expert, or that a peasant should carry out operations while the surgeon cleaned the hospital toilets. Tony Blair recounted that in a debate one day, an angry dissenter shouted 'So you know more about everything than I do!' Tony Blair replied calmly, 'Well I know a certain number of things because I was prime minister for ten years'. This is only common sense, but it didn't seem to occur to the person concerned.

This was the first wake-up call – astonishing *a priori* in a country whose DNA seemed the most liberal, enthusiastic about free trade and pragmatic, with a tradition of openness and tolerance. A country which was a leading advocate for globalisation, from which it was benefitting through strong economic growth and full employment despite a policy of austerity. However, already there was a conflict between people from 'somewhere'[1] (those on the fringe, as it were) and people from 'anywhere' (internationalists and city-dwellers, or as Theresa May called them after her victory, 'citizens of nowhere' who can live and work in Paris, New York, London, Singapore or Hong Kong). The election of Donald Trump followed along similar lines, based on this same hatred of the establishment on the part of frustrated citizens living in areas whose industries were in decline and who felt left behind by globalisation. I followed the result of the presidential election of November 2016 at the American Embassy and very quickly had the feeling of living through Brexit night again. Even before the final result, the impression was that nothing was going as expected in the various states. Even late into the evening, the prediction was still that Hillary Clinton would win. I left before the end but continued to follow the results through the night. All the Americans living in London and those passing through had for months been telling me that a victory for Trump was impossible, if only for arithmetical reasons (women + Black + Latino voters, etc). Wrong again. Having lived through Brexit, I was less surprised this time around. The British were torn between astonishment and a certain *Schadenfreude,* relief at not having been the only ones to have 'fucked up'. The Brexiteers rejoiced openly and Nigel Farage – possibly the most narrowly parochial man in the United Kingdom – hurried to Trump Tower in New York where, supported by a private fund, he started to organise a new life for himself in the United States, a project which, in the end, he abandoned.

Thus began the *'affolement du monde'*[ii,2] – the Trump fairground shooting gallery, the unreal and at times surreal world of Brexitland (lampooned in the tweets of Alex Taylor, an English journalist, naturalised French, who nearly always began with '*Je n'invente pas*' – 'I'm not making this up'[3]), Salvini's unlikely coalition in Italy, the return to the Bundestag of the far-right (AfD) in Germany which we thought was immune, then the *gilets jaunes* in France who imagined they were living in a totalitarian state.

A common feature on both sides of the Atlantic is that the underprivileged and frustrated were prepared to hand over the keys of their destiny to a man who, in reality, belongs to the detested elite but who has the gift of being able to convince the gullible amongst them that he is their mouthpiece, a man of the people, like them. By feeding them false information and provoking anxiety – in relation to the European Union and immigrants, in the case of the UK – populist leaders have cleverly manipulated the

---

[ii] This French expression has a mixture of two meanings here: 'descent into chaos', and also 'panic on the part of the leaders'.

people. They then declare themselves to be the sole protectors of the 'sacred' will of the people, refusing to recognise any other viewpoint or intermediary. As Mirabeau (a leader of the early stages of the French Revolution) put it *'Nous sommes ici par la volonté du peuple et n'en sortirons, par la force des baïonnettes'* – 'We are here by the will of the people and will succeed only through armed struggle'. Those who do not share their dogmatic view of the world are branded as capitulators, traitors or enemies of the people, and exposed in the tabloids to public hatred.

Is there indeed such a thing as a coherent 'will of the people'? In the specific case of Brexit, no one ever succeeded in defining it, beyond that it involved leaving the European Union. Who is to decide? The billionaire and all-powerful press baron Rupert Murdoch, despite being a 'foreigner'? By what magic trick did old Etonians and graduates from Oxford – by very definition, core members of the establishment – succeed in passing themselves off convincingly as suitable candidates to represent anti-establishment voters? How is it that their disguise was not penetrated during the months or years following? Why such gullibility or indulgence? There was a time in politics when a lie – exposed as such – was a cardinal sin. Today, in the 'post-truth' era, the more you lie, the more popular you become. However, the calamitous mismanagement of the coronavirus epidemic by populist leaders living in denial who, in some cases, finished up in hospital, has meant that questions are beginning to be asked. Will this continue to be the case? What does seem to be permanent is the growing division between populations and countries, in most of which there is a split between the urban and the elite on the one hand, and those who have been described as 'peripheral' – populations living in small towns with declining industries and in rural areas – on the other. Such division is no doubt set to continue with Joe Biden versus the continuing resistance of Trump supporters. For its part, the world is divided as never before between democracies and illiberal regimes, or quasi-dictatorships.

Paul Morand wondered what London – which he described in the 1930s as his mascot – would be like in the future.[4] With prescience, he predicted that it would 'rise skywards thanks to steel and concrete [...] soon its suburbs will find themselves at the entrance to a tunnel under the Channel. Closer to Paris than are Lyons or Bordeaux, London will be subject to the direct influence of the continent from which it had thought itself, since the Renaissance, to be definitively detached.' He wondered if London would be 'the centre of a large empire or its subsidiary, [...] a denationalised capital with a Canadian prime minister, Australian press, New Zealand novels, Rhodesian music, speaking Afrikaans'. It's funny to think that in 2016, the Governor of the Bank of England was indeed Canadian and the media in the hands of an Australian magnate. Or else, he wondered, 'would the large dominions, like ripe fruits, have fallen from the tree leaving London a retirement home, a peaceful Holland of traditions and museums, next to its Westminster Abbey'. I read this lovely little book, entitled simply *Londres*, on my arrival in the United Kingdom when the reply was obvious, but today the destiny of the country is again uncertain.

So, what next? Knowing now that other 'black swans' can come along and change the course of events. The British are not people who cry over spilt milk. They will bounce back, for they are dynamic and also have the gift of being able to transform failure into something mythical – 'heroic failure' as the Irish journalist Fintan O'Toole puts it so well with reference to George Orwell, using many graphic examples such as the *Charge of the Light Brigade*, or the tragedy of Gordon in Khartoum, Dunkirk.[5] The liberal Boris Johnson, who dreamt of a deregulated economy is embarking on a Keynesian programme of recovery through investment in infrastructure projects. Those who listened to the sirens of the leading Brexiteers have accepted that they will be poorer, but for how long will such a declaration of principle hold out against the principle of reality? To be free and independent, to take back control, but how is this to be achieved given that the UK is caught between the competing and very strong pressures from the Chinese and American giants? Will it be enough, as proclaimed by Boris Johnson, to have faith in one's country? Although the agreement was approved by the Westminster

Parliament in haste on 30 December 2020, the opposition of the Lib Dems, the DUP and (above all) the SNP shows that the divisions have not gone away. For Scotland, the wish for a second referendum will not disappear, but there is a greater likelihood of Ireland being reunified – the right is in the constitution and cannot be prevented by Westminster. Already, the special status of Northern Ireland, still aligned with some European rules, means that there is greater co-operation between Belfast and Dublin in certain areas.

The economy apart, what will be the UK's relationship with the European Union as regards security, defence, the sharing of information, scientific exchanges and adhesion to the EU's diplomatic positions? 'No man [or country] is an island' wrote the English poet John Donne in the 17th century. This is all the more true in these days of globalisation which will no doubt continue despite protectionist temptations. Will the next generations be tempted to rejoin the EU? Everything will depend on the balance of power, impossible to predict at this stage, and the capacity of the European Union to go further down the road of economic integration in order to be credible and assert itself as a political power. The new understanding between Macron and Merkel would seem to pave the way for this. The European Union undoubtedly scored points at the end of the year with the Brexit agreement, which protected the single market and the interests of its citizens, a policy of buying vaccines in bulk and therefore relatively cheaply, and the conclusion of an agreement on investment with China without timidly waiting for approval from Washington. The possibility of a United States-China-European Union triumvirate would thus seem to have a promising future. It's true that much remains to be done – we are talking about 'work in progress' – but the way ahead seems to be clear even though, as the French poet Aragon said, *'rien n'est jamais acquis à l'homme, ni sa force, ni sa faiblesse.'*[iii]

[iii] 'Nothing is ever definitively acquired by man [or in this case, a country, or the European Union], neither his strength nor his weakness.'

Endnotes

Preface

1   Stephens, P, *Britain Alone: The Path from Suez to Brexit*, Faber & Faber, 2021.
2   Ricketts, P, *Hard Choices: What Britain Does Next*, Atlantic Books, 2021.

Introduction

1   Carrol, L, *Alice in Wonderland*, Macmillan, 1865.
2   Morand, P, *Londres/Le Noveau Londres*, Gallimard, 2012.
3   Coe, J, *Middle England*, Viking Press, 2018.
4   Vincent, B, *Five on Brexit Island*, Quercus, 2016.
5   Young, L, *Alice in Brexitland*, Ebury Press, 2017.
6   McEwan, I, *The Cockroach*, Vintage Books, 2019.
7   le Carré, J, *Agent Running in the Field*, Viking Press, 2019.
8   Brookes, P, *The Red Carpet to No. 10, The Times*, 12 July 2016.
9   Oliver, C, *Unleashing Demons: The Inside Story of Brexit*, Hodder & Stoughton, 2016.
10   Peston, R, *WTF?*, Hodder & Stoughton, 2017.
11   As reported on BBC *News*, 8 November 2020.
12   Diamanti, I, and Lazar, M, *Peuplecratie: la métamorphose de nos démocraties*, Gallimard, 2019.
13   'Scottish independence: Yes leads by 53% to 47%', *yougov.co.uk*, 2020.
14   Allison, G, *Destined for War: Can America and China Escape Thucydides' Trap?*, Scribe Publishing Company, 2017.
15   Thucydides, *The Peloponnesian War*, Hackett Publishing, 1998.
16   Badie, B, *Nous ne sommes plus seuls au monde*, La Découverte, 2016.

Chapter 1

1   Coe, J, *Number 11*, Viking Press, 2015.
2   Hollingsworth, M, and Langley, S, *Londongrad: From Russia with Cash*, Fourth Estate Ltd, 2010.
3   Ashcroft, M, and Oakeshott, I, *Call Me Dave*, Biteback Publishing, 2015.

4   'Prince Charles's "black spider memos" show lobbying at highest political level', *The Guardian*, 2015.
5   Roche, M, *Elle ne voulait pas être reine!*, Albin Michel, 2020.
6   Gravier, JF, *Paris et le désert français*, Le Portulan, 1947.

Chapter 2

1   Shakespeare, W, *Richard II*, 1597.
2   'Heavy Fog in the Channel. Continent Cut Off', *The Times*, 1957.
3   Marshall, HE, *Our Island Story*, TC & EC Jack, 1905.
4   Low, D, *Very Well, Alone, The Evening Standard,* 1940.
5   Johnson, B, *The Churchill Factor,* Hodder & Stoughton, 2014.
6   Zeldin, T, *A History of French Passions*, Oxford University Press, 1973–77.
7   O'Toole, F, *Heroic Failure: Brexit and the Politics of Pain*, Head of Zeus, 2018.
8   O'Rourke, K, *A Short History of Brexit*, Pelican, 2019.
9   Disraeli, B, as quoted by Thatcher, M, in 'Speech to Conservative Group for Europe (opening Conservative referendum campaign), Thatcher Archive: CCOPR 314/75; ITN Archive: *News at Ten*, 16 April 1975.
10 Churchill, W, as quoted in Tombs, R, and Chabal, E, *Britain and France in Two World Wars: Truth, Myth and Memory*, Bloomsbury, 2013.
11 Sopel, J, *If Only They Didn't Speak English: Notes From Trump's America*, Ebury Publishing, 2017.

Chapter 3

1   Tombs, R, and Tombs, I, *That Sweet Enemy*, Pimlico, 2007.
2   Clemenceau, G, as quoted in Janvrin, I, and Rawlinson, C, *The French in London*, Bitter Lemon Press, 2016.
3   'Battle of Hastings (2016) gives black eye to anti-Europe feeling', *Financial Times*, 14 October 2016.
4   Carroll, L, *Alice's Adventures in Wonderland*, Macmillan, 1865.
5   Christophe, *La Famille Fenouillard*, 1893.
6   Clarke, S, *1000 Years of Annoying the French*, Transworld, 2015 [2010].
7   Clarke, S, *How the French won Waterloo (or Think They Did)*, Cornerstone, 2015.

Chapter 4

1   'Penny Mordaunt: "The UK can't veto Turkey joining EU"', *BBC News*, 22 May 2016.
2   Shakespeare, W, *The Tempest*, Act I Scene II, 1611.

Chapter 5

1 Cato the Younger, *Guilty Men: Brexit Edition*, Biteback Publishing, 2017.
2 Maurois, A, *Les Anglais*, Cahiers Libres, 1927.
3 Cameron, David, *For the Record*, Harper Collins UK, 2019.
4 Cameron, David, *For the Record*, op cit.
5 Hazley, JA, and Morris, JP, *The Story of Brexit*, Ladybird Books Ltd, 2018.
6 'Emma Barnett's interview with Jeremy Corbyn fuels Labour anti-semitism row', *The Times*, 2017.

Chapter 6

1 'Being a mother gives me edge on May – Leadsom', *The Times*, 9 July 2016.
2 Rogers, I, *9 Lessons in Brexit*, Short Books, 2019.
3 'Parliament finally has its say: No. No. No. No. No. No. No. No' *The Guardian*, 28 March 2019.
4 'Queen Opens Parliament', *Private Eye*, 20 October 1964.
5 'Ditch Speaks Out', *Private Eye*, 1 November 2019.

Chapter 7

1 'Farewell to the EU', *The Times*, 1 February 2020.
2 'Boris Exclusive on his Hospital Hell: Docs Were Ready For Me To Die', *The Sun*, 2 May 2020.
3 Gimson, A, *Boris*, Simon & Schuster, 2016.
4 Body, G, for *The New Zealand Herald*, 3 February 2020.
5 Fang, F, *Wuhan Diary*, Harper Collins, 2020.
6 Mahbubani, K, *Has the West lost?*, Allen Lane, 2018.
7 Mahbubani, K, *Has China Won?*, Public Affairs, 2020.

Afterword

1 Goodhart, D, *The Road to Somewhere*, Penguin Books, 2017.
2 Gomart, T, *L'Affolement du monde*, Tallandier, 2020.
3 Taylor, A, *Brexit: L'autopsie d'une illusion*, JC Lattès, 2019.
4 Morand, P, *Londres/Le Noveau Londres*, Gallimard, 2012.
5 O'Toole, F, *Heroic Failure: Brexit and the Politics of Pain*, Head of Zeus, 2018.

Bibliography

Non-fiction

Allison, G, *Destined for War: Can America and China Escape Thucydides' Trap?*, Scribe, 2017.

Badie, B, *Nous ne sommes plus seuls au monde*, La Découverte, 2016.

Barber, L, *The powerful and the damned: private diaries in turbulent times*, WH Allen, 2020.

Barnett, A, *The Lure of Greatness: England's Brexit and America's Trump*, Penguin, 2017.

'Battle of Hastings (2016) gives black eye to anti-Europe feeling', *Financial Times*, 14 October 2016.

'Being a mother gives me edge on May – Leadsom', *The Times*, 9 July 2016.

'Boris Exclusive on his Hospital Hell: Docs Were Ready For Me To Die', *The Sun*, 2 May 2020.

Cameron, D, *For the Record*, Harper Collins UK, 2019.

Cato the Younger, *Guilty Men*, Brexit Edition, Biteback Publishing 2017.

Churchill, W, as quoted in Tombs, R, and Chabal, E, *Britain and France in Two World Wars: Truth, Myth and Memory*, Bloomsbury, 2013.

Clarke, S, *1000 Years of Annoying the French*, Century, 2010.

— *How the French Won Waterloo*, Century, 2015.

Clemenceau, G, as quoted in Janvrin, I, and Rawlinson, C, *The French in London*, Bitter Lemon Press, 2016.

Diamanti, I, and Lazar, M, *Peuplecratie. La métamorphose de nos démocraties*, Gallimard, 2019.

Disraeli, B, as quoted by Thatcher, M, in 'Speech to Conservative Group for Europe (opening Conservative referendum campaign), Thatcher Archive: CCOPR 314/75; ITN Archive: *News at Ten*, 16 April 1975.

'Ditch Speaks Out', *Private Eye*, 1 November 2019.

'Emma Barnett's interview with Jeremy Corbyn fuels Labour antisemitism row', *The Times*, 2017.

Enderlin, S, *Angleterre, Brexit et conséquences*, Nevicata, 2017.

Fang, F, *Wuhan Diary*, Harper Collins, 2020.

'Farewell to the EU', *The Times*, 1 February 2020.

Gimson, A, *Boris: The Making of the Prime Minster*, Simon & Schuster, 2016.

Gomart, T, *L'Affolement du monde. 10 enjeux géopolitiques*, Tallandier, 2019.

Goodhart, D, *The Road to Somewhere: The Populist Revolt and the Future of Politics*, Penguin 2017.

Gravier, JF, *Paris et le désert français*, Le Portulan, 1947.

Hazeley, JA, and Morris JP, *The Story of Brexit*, Ladybird Books Ltd.

'Heavy Fog in the Channel. Continent Cut Off', *The Times*, 1957.

Hollingsworth, M, and Langley, S, *Londongrad: From Russia with Cash*, Fourth Estate Ltd, 2010.

Janvrin, I, and Rawlinson, C, *Les Français à Londres: de Guillaume le Conquérant à Charles de Gaulle*, Editions Bibliomane, 2013.

Johnson, B, *The Churchill Factor*, Hodder & Stoughton, 2014.

Kelly, L, *Talleyrand in London: The Master Diplomat's Last Mission*, IB Tauris, 2017.

Mahbubani, K, *Has the West Lost?*, Allen Lane, 2018.

— *Has China Won? The Chinese Challenge to American Primacy*, Public Affairs, 2020.

Müller, JW, *What is Populism?*, Penguin, 2017.

Oakeshott, I, and Ashcroft, M, *Call me Dave*, Biteback Publishing, 2015.

Oliver, C, *Unleashing Demons: The Inside Story of Brexit*, Hodder & Stoughton, 2016.

O'Rourke, K, *A Short History of Brexit*, Pelican, 2019.

O'Toole, F, *Heroic Failure: Brexit and the Politics of Pain*, Head of Zeus, 2018.

'Parliament finally has its say: No. No. No. No. No. No. No', *The Guardian*, 28 March 2019.

'Penny Mordaunt: "The UK can't veto Turkey joining EU"', BBC News, 22 May 2016.

Peston, R, *WTF?: What have we done? Why did it happen? How do we take back control?*, Hodder & Stoughton, 2017.

'Prince Charles's "black spider memos" show lobbying at highest political level', *The Guardian*, 2015.

'Queen Opens Parliament', *Private Eye*, 20 October 1964.

Roche, M, *Le Brexit va réussir*, Albin Michel, 2018.

— *Elle ne voulait pas être reine!*, Albin Michel, 2020.

Rogers, I, *9 Lessons in Brexit*, Short Books, 2019.

'Scottish independence: Yes leads by 53% to 47%', yougov.co.uk, 2020.

Shipman, T, *All Out War: The Full Story of How Brexit Sank Britain's Political Class*, William Collins, 2016.

— *Fall Out: A Year of Political Mayhem*, William Collins, 2018.

Sopel, J, *If Only They Didn't Speak English*, BBC Books, 2017.

Taylor, A, *Brexit. L'autopsie d'une illusion*, Lattès, 2019.

Tharoor, S, *Inglorious Empire: What the British Did to India*, Hurst, 2019.

Thucydide, *La Guerre du Péloponnèse*, Les Belles Lettres, 1990.

Tombs, R, *The English and their History*, Penguin, 2015.

Tombs, I, Tombs, R, *That Sweet Enemy*, Pimlico, 2007.

Trierweiler, V, *Thank You For This Moment: A Story of Love, Power and Betrayal*, Biteback, 2014.

Van Reterghem, M, *Mon Europe, je t'aime moi non plus*, Stock, 2019.

Zeldin, T, *A History of French Passions*, Oxford University Press, 1973–77.

— *Les Français*, Fayard, 1983.

Fiction

Caroll, L, *Alice's Adventures in Wonderland*, Macmillan, 1865.

Coe, J, *Number 11*, Viking Press, 2015.

— *Middle England*, Viking Press, 2018.

Christophe, *La Famille Fenouillard*, 1893.

Le Carré, J, *Agent Running in the Field*, Viking Press, 2019.

Marshall, HE, *Our Island Story: A History of Britain for Boys and Girls*, Weidenfeld & Nicolson, 2014 (TC & EC Jack, 1905).

McEwan, I, *The Cockroach*, Vintage Publishing, 2019.

Morand, P, *Londres* followed by *Le Nouveau Londres*, Gallimard, 2012.

Shakespeare, W, *Richard II*, 1623.

Vincent, Bruno, *Five on Brexit Island,* Quercus, 2016.

Young, L, *Alice in Brexitland*, Ebury Press, 2017.

Cartoons

Benson, T (editor), *Britain's Best Political Cartoons,* Hutchinson, Annual publication.

Brookes, P, 'The Red Carpet to No. 10', *The Times*, 12 July 2016.

Body, G, for *The New Zealand Herald*, 3 February 2020.

Goscinny and Uderzo, *Astérix*, Dargaud.

Low, D, 'Very Well, Alone', *The Evening Standard*, 1940.

Filmography

Cinema, Television, Theatre

Cinema

Allen, W, *Match Point*, 2005

Frears, S, *The Queen*, 2006

Hooper, T, *The King's Speech*, 2010

Jones, T, *Monty Python. Life of Brian,* 1979 (for the parallel with the EU in the cult scene — '*What have the Romans ever done for us?*')

Loach, K, *I, Daniel Blake*, 2016

Nolan, C, *Dunkirk*, 2017

Wright, J, *Darkest Hour*, 2017

Television

Davies, A, *House of Cards*, BBC, 1990, 1993, 1995

Davies, R, *Years and Years*, BBC, 2019

Graham, J, *Brexit: The Uncivil War*, Channel 4, 2019

Jay, A, and Lynn, J, *Yes Minister*, BBC 1980–1982 and *Yes Prime Minister*, BBC, 1986–1988

Morgan, P, *The Crown*, Netflix, 2016–

Perry, J, and Croft, D, *Dad's Army*, 1968–1977

Theatre

Graham, J, *This House*, 2017 (directed by Jeremy Herrin)

Morgan, P, *The Audience*, 2013–

Luath Press Limited

committed to publishing well written books worth reading

LUATH PRESS takes its name from Robert Burns, whose little collie Luath (*Gael.*, swift or nimble) tripped up Jean Armour at a wedding and gave him the chance to speak to the woman who was to be his wife and the abiding love of his life. Burns called one of the 'Twa Dogs' Luath after Cuchullin's hunting dog in Ossian's *Fingal*. Luath Press was established in 1981 in the heart of Burns country, and is now based a few steps up the road from Burns' first lodgings on Edinburgh's Royal Mile. Luath offers you distinctive writing with a hint of unexpected pleasures.

Most bookshops in the UK, the US, Canada, Australia, New Zealand and parts of Europe, either carry our books in stock or can order them for you. To order direct from us, please send a £sterling cheque, postal order, international money order or your credit card details (number, address of cardholder and expiry date) to us at the address below. Please add post and packing as follows: UK – £1.00 per delivery address; overseas surface mail – £2.50 per delivery address; overseas airmail – £3.50 for the first book to each delivery address, plus £1.00 for each additional book by airmail to the same address. If your order is a gift, we will happily enclose your card or message at no extra charge.

Luath Press Limited
543/2 Castlehill
The Royal Mile
Edinburgh EH1 2ND
Scotland
Telephone: +44 (0)131 225 4326 (24 hours)
email: sales@luath. co.uk
Website: www. luath.co.uk